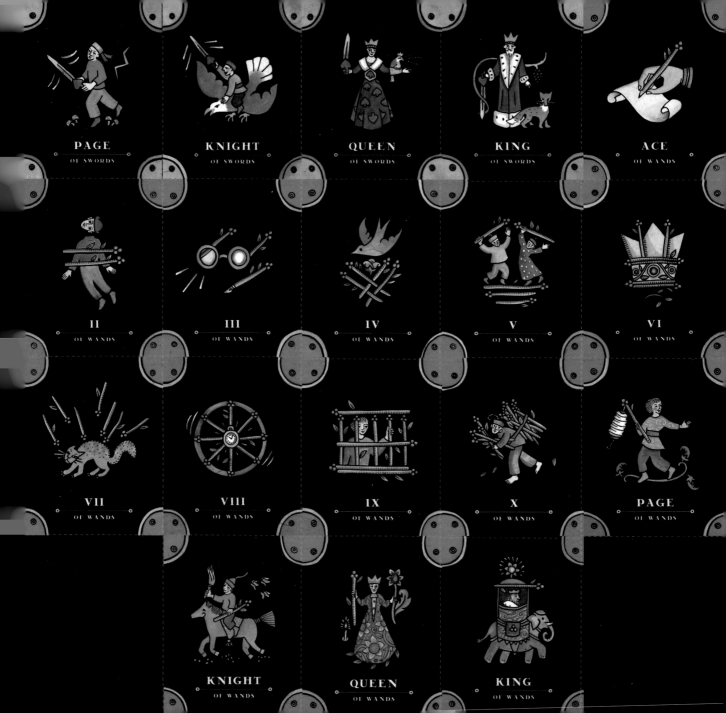

THE
FORTUNE
TELLING
HANDBOOK

The Interactive Guide to Tarot, Palm Reading, and More

by Dennis Fairchild

Illustrated by Julie Paschkis

RUNNING PRESS

PHILADELPHIA · LONDON

© 2003 by Dennis Fairchild
Illustrations © 2003 by Julie Paschkis

All rights reserved under the Pan-American and International Copyright Conventions
Printed in the United States

9 8 7 6 5 4 3 2 1

Digit on the right indicates the number of this printing

Library of Congress Cataloging-in-Publication Number 2002108930
ISBN 0-7624-1444-8

Designed by Corinda Cook
Edited by Deborah Grandinetti
Illustrations by Julie Paschkis
Typography: Granjon and Greco Deco

This book may be ordered by mail from the publisher.
Please include $2.50 for postage and handling.
But try your bookstore first!

Running Press Book Publishers
125 South Twenty-second Street
Philadelphia, Pennsylvania 19103-4399

Visit us on the web!
www.runningpress.com

CONTENTS

INTRODUCTION

I see the Past, Present and Future existing all at once before me.

—William Blake

Back when Ike was President and most little boys read Tom Swift or The Hardy Boys, I grew up reading palms and stars.

My Grandma was a well-known clairvoyant-astrologer for the inner circles of politicos, governors, presidents, and rich and famous types. She was wary of generic supermarket tabloid stargazing stuff, although her galpals were the likes of Sybil Leek, Jeane Dixon and other featured futurists.

At an early age, she tutored me in the arts of Forecasting, which got me thinking more about "cosmic" events than the Clearasil I needed, and more about astrology than algebra. She predicted my prom night "results" rather than the presidential election.

Decades after my acne took a hike, I matured into what is commonly called a "fortune-teller." I am a full-time handwriting analyst, palmist, tarot card reader, astrologer, and numerologist.

Today, everyone remains curious about the Future. This book reveals how to put a finger on the pulse of tomorrows-to-come. So close the refrigerator door, open up your mind, and please allow me to be *your* surrogate psychic grandparent.

CHAPTER ONE

TRY YOUR HAND AT GRAPHOLOGY

> **Then all the King's wise men came in,**
> **but they could not read the writing or tell what it meant.**
>
> —Daniel 5:8

Handwriting reveals your thoughts and feelings the instant you put pen to paper. Written sentences resemble an EEG—an electroencephalogram—the modern device for recording brainwaves. Handwriting does not predict your future. It is an excellent objective diagnostic tool for exploring character and personality, however. It's said that character breeds destiny.

Before launching a consultation, I provide sheets of unlined paper and ask clients to write a brief self-addressed letter about their hopes and dreams or projects for the weeks ahead. Do the same yourself in the space provided below:

Next, note the following, step-by-step:

IS THE WRITING SAMPLE:

Sloppy or Illegible, Rushed-looking? If so, you have a rather complicated and tricky mind. You usually do things in roundabout or involved ways instead of being simple and direct. To be successful, you need the self-discipline of persistence. Your mind changes courses quickly, and you go from idea to idea. Establish definite objectives and construct a positive plan for realizing them.

Clear and Calculated? You try to be extremely careful, and take great pride in making something as nearly perfect as possible. You are able to solve problems easily because you use every fragment of information available. Your conservative mentality allows you to accomplish a great deal with the least amount of effort. Knowing your limits, you confine your objectives within them. Be careful not to be so critical that you only see flaws.

How Far from the Schoolroom Model Does the Writing Deviate? When your writing strongly resembles that of a class book, you tend to be conventional, careful in everything you do and aware of society's dictates. When you deviate from the writing style in which you were drilled, you want to be yourself and you may resist anything or anyone who tries to make you conform to a standard you can't swallow. Nevertheless, because you are open and forthright, others will respect you.

Sloppy or Illegible

Clear and Calculated

Deviate from schoolbook

WHAT PAGE PLACEMENT TELLS YOU

Because we write from left to right and top to bottom as we move across the page, the left and top represents the past, while the right and bottom suggests the future. Where and how are your words placed on the page? Are the words placed so that they:

Hug the Left with a Wide Right Margin? You put up imaginary barriers as to how far you can get in life and tend to cling to the past (or your momma). You may get into routines or habits you fear to break, for you prefer familiar and known ways of doing things. Don't be an emotional patsy for those who brutalize you emotionally with their guilt and incompetence.

Provide an Overly Wide Left Margin? This trait signals someone with an unpleasant past from which they are eager to flee. Future-minded, you try never to let a narrow point of view keep you from fully understanding the world. Discovery brings you pleasure, although you may have a tendency to dream too much about tomorrow rather than tending to necessities of the moment.

Fill Page after Page with No Margins? You feel that you must fill every waking moment with activity. Compulsive, mentally busy and a bit of a financial tightwad. Your mind races eagerly as you seek answers because you cannot tolerate sitting still or being ignorant.

Provide a Wide Upper Margin? You respect others, understand formality. You try to solve problems logically and are cautious about voicing your opinions in conversation. Tradition and custom represent security, which you admire.

Create a Narrow Upper Margin? You have a tendency to bow down to others, not speak up for yourself. You overdramatize others' qualities and underestimate your own. You have a strong desire to be useful to people you deal with and are flexible enough to make allowances for them.

Hugging Left with Wide Right Margin

Overly Wide Left Margin

Fills Page with No Margins

Wide Upper Margin

Narrow Upper Margin

My favorite season is summer. What is your favorite time of the year? I like to go to the beach, enjoying the sunshine and the water. I also enjoy going sailing on the bay.

It is exciting to go camping and take hikes in the mountains. The lush outdoors exhilarates and delights me. When I enjoy nature, I challenge myself in many ways.

1.

2.

Wide Lower Margin

this strangled writing and no spacing

Sentences tangle together like barbed wire

I'm quite precise, like an architect

Sentences flow Clear and Straight

I really like you!

Smooth, Alive and Active

I really like you!

Calculated, hesitant in Appearance

Create a Wide Lower Margin? You find it difficult to let go of the past and anyone associated with it. You are apprehensive about the future, "adjusting" hopes and dreams to what is emotionally tolerable to you. Try to examine situations intellectually and judge them fairly. Be realistic in your goals.

EXAMINING HOW WHOLE SENTENCES LOOK

Do Sentences Tangle Together like Barbed Wire? You may be a bit of a chatterbox and find it as difficult to express yourself clearly as to understand what others are saying. Your nervous thinking often keeps you confused by feelings and imagination. Examine situations and yourself intellectually and fairly. An impressible person, you have difficulty in realistically evaluating situations. If you are wrong: admit it!

Do Sentences Flow Clear and Straight Like an Engineer's Blueprint? Common sense and experience are very important to you when decision-making. You think carefully and arrive at conclusions only after much thought. You like ideas and objects to be neat and orderly.

DOES THE SPEED AND FLOW OF THE WRITING LOOK:

Smooth, Alive and Active? Your personality is quite varied and exciting because your emotional responses are accompanied by intellectual curiosity. Although you are affectionate and enjoy being loved, you want to be free—emotionally and otherwise, not tied down.

Calculated, Hesitant in Appearance? Very little escapes your notice. You are slow and careful in your thinking, because you want to know all the facts before making a decision, and even then you take your time. Because you feel that emotions must be understood before any conflict can be resolved, you may feel that you are alone when you are really not.

HOW ARE THE WORDS PLACED?

Space between words represents the amount of emotional and physical distance the writer needs in order to feel comfortable with others. Each word you write represents ego. Where you place the next word suggests where you subconsciously choose to put other people in relationship to yourself.

Are There Large Spaces Between Each Word? If so, it's difficult for you to share your feelings with others; you tend to be a loner who prefers to be by yourself. You are much happier in small groups rather than large gatherings. In crowds, you are likely to feel much lonelier than when you are really alone. Seek to overcome your feeling of distance by finding out and emphasizing what you and others have in common.

Do Words Run Together with Only a Tight Space in Between? Narrow word spacing suggests that you don't need much elbow room or approval from others. You're not afraid of being yourself in social situations. Even people who don't like something you are doing admire the spirit in which you do it. Those you like rarely doubt your feelings.

DOES THE WRITING:

Slant Downwards? (Think "sinking ship.") Sentences that descend reveal a person who is less hopeful, inclined to be somber or pessimistic . . . although not necessarily morbid or suicidal. You may feel unloved and remote, reluctant to trust others with your emotions because you often feel misunderstood. You need emotional support and care just as much as anybody else does, although you may be unwilling to admit it. Don't feel rejected or sorry for yourself. Clear up depression by stopping sulking and finding out why the problem developed in the first place!

Ascend? (Think "airplane taking off") Normally, you have a positive, optimistic and open-minded outlook on life and conduct yourself with decorum. You respond to honesty and gravitate towards persons

This is wide spacing

Large spaces between each word

I really like you!

Words run together with tight spaces between

I think you're nice.

Slant downwards

you're the best.

Words ascend

with that quality. Even when you get depressed, you don't stay that way for long. Your ability to not take yourself or life too seriously helps you snap out of bad moods quickly.

LOOKING AT THE OVERALL SHAPE

What "shape" prevails in your handscript? Repetitious symbols—circle, square, jagged or erratic—provide clues about general disposition. The four primary formations are called Arcades, Angles, Garlands, and Threads.

Arcades resemble the rounded humps of a camel. The more predominant the bump, the more reserved, traditional and protective you tend to be. You do things carefully and thoroughly and hate to overlook steps. You are slow in your thinking because you want to know all the facts before making decisions—and, even then, you take your time. You are conservative, preferring to deal with familiar ideas. Beware of a tendency to be overly secretive. Make friends with your feelings!

Angular writing looks like lightning bolts or pointy pine trees blowing in a strong wind and points to decisiveness, purposeful goal-making. More intellectual or factual rather than emotional, dreamy. You put together ideas that to others seem unrelated. You're good at planning and organizing and put all of the pieces of the puzzle together to make a whole; you are able to see and understand all elements of a situation. You learn very well. However, note that an abundance of strong-slanting Angles reveal rigidity and inflexibility.

Garland writing resembles the U-shaped like the lower arc of a circle. Garland-writers are noncompetitive, passive people who like people. You are very sociable and enjoy good company and good times, not harshness. You are an excellent team player. Your concern in getting along makes you put the interests of the group above your own, although you usually feel that they are the same. However, sometimes you are unsure whether to assert yourself, give way to the other's demands, or compromise, although the first can be the most difficult choice of the three.

minutes, imagination

Arcades

Forget it!

Angular

I love you

Garland

12

Thread-like handwriting, formless like a snake's movement in sand and characterized by indistinct formations combining the Arcade and Garland isn't entirely straight nor curvy, but a little of each. The thready writer is generally unassertive, sensitive, highly impressionable and fast thinking. You have a quick mind and can understand ideas that others can't, because you are open to new options. When confronted with a puzzle or challenging problem, you solve it rapidly, seeking fast solutions. But without self-control you will not carry out ideas far enough; you will go to a new area before you have thought out the first one. In any case, keep away from situations that will make you overexcited or competitive.

Thread-like

ANALYZING THE UPPER ZONE

Handwriting also divides letters and script into three horizontal "Zones." Each represents a specific part of the writer's personality. Note the dominant image: are Zones balanced, one overly embellished? For overall personality balance, all three should be equally represented. When one predominates, it is at the expense of the other two.

The Upper Zone concerns knowledge, ideas, imagination, mental pursuits. Upper Zone letters have extensions rising above from their middle: b, d, f, h, k, l, t. Letters or parts of letters that balloon upwards where they don't belong deserve special attention. Too much exaggeration here—whether by flourishes or loops—suggesting difficulty functioning in some area of the real world.

Bloated Upper Zone Writing reveals a hearty ego and strongly developed concepts of who you are. You ask a great deal out of life in terms of goals and material possessions. You are an idealist who wants the world to be quite different or to revolve around you. When dealing with others, you have to be especially careful that you see them as they really are—as well as yourself! Aim to keep other people's needs in mind with your own.

Bloated Upper Zone

Overly Balloon-like upper zone

Thin Twig-like upper zone

Minuscule, Wimpy upper zone

Lower zone inflated

Deflated lower zone

Overly Balloon-Like Upper Zone suggests that your imagination runs rampant. You may act in hasty, rash ways that you may later regret. You are a free thinker and cannot stand to be confined or restricted. Your air of self-importance is huge.

Thin Twig-Like Upper Zone Script reveals an unexpansive thinker with little room for options. (Were you raised in an authoritarian, narrow-minded household?) You insist on a strict code of behavior for yourself and others. You like to learn, but only in structured settings. If you cannot see the tradition or usefulness of something, you are not likely to find much value in it.

Minuscule, Wimpy Upper Zones aren't interested in others' values and rarely have strong spiritual or religious beliefs. You play down your feelings and concentrate on other avenues. You may resist doing something for fun when others would hate to pass up a good time. You prefer living outside the painful pressures that characterize the "rat race."

ANALYZING THE LOWER ZONE

The Lower Zone deals with sexual and material desires (as well as how you repress them). Does the Lower Zone rule? Is it inflated, large? If so, then the physical and material desires are given more emphasis than the social or mental. When you want something, you will do everything in your power to obtain it, which may lead to conflicts if you are not careful. You're sensual, don't like being held down or disciplined, are careful of becoming too possessive of friends or belongings. It may be easier for you to remain detached than have your needs denied; don't fret over rejection or keeping up with The Joneses. (You're probably an envious sort, and have an amazing fantasy life!)

Deflated, Compressed and Thin Lower Zone Script suggests self-sufficiency and independence combined with feelings of guilt, gossip, unfulfilled sexuality or issues with mom that may have spilled over to

other women (especially if the script aims to the left). You use your energy efficiently, wasting little of it on nonproductive efforts. You aren't preoccupied with power as an instrument for gain but see it rather as a force for continued growth.

Neglected Lower Zone Strokes say that you may fear closeness in social or sexual encounters and have trouble opening up to people. Your ties to the past and emotional securities may not align with the ways in which you consciously express your will and desire. Freedom is very important and you resist those who may try to fence you in. Hard work brings you the results you crave.

ANALYZING THE MIDDLE ZONE

One's Middle Zone integrates the intellectual/spiritual (Upper Zone) with the material and sexual (Lower Zone). When the writing of the Middle Zone is emphasized at the expense of the others, the writer lives in the here and now and is very concerned about practical, everyday matters. Any desire to assert yourself on impulse is balanced by realization of the consequences of such actions. This quality of restraint can mean great accomplishments for you because you don't waste energy on unproductive efforts. You represent the "ideal" in terms of a balance between aggression and self-control.

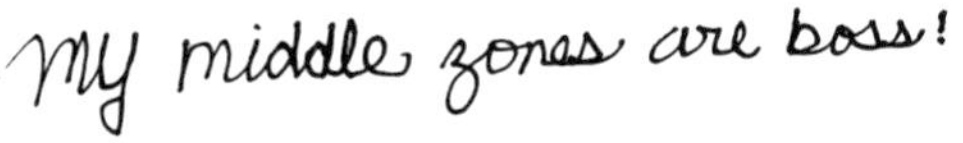

Is the Middle Zone Dwarfed? You fluctuate between knowing what you are worth to having grave doubts about your abilities to assist others or may make promises that you can't fulfill. You choose to live in your own little world, ignoring what's happening on CNN. Bone up on self-esteem and don't bite off more than you can digest. After some experience, you'll earn the pats on your back and social securities that you seek.

Zero lower zone – zippo

Neglected lower zone

my middle zones are boss!

Middle zone emphasized

O baly !

Middle zone dwarfed

15

Here I go: straight

Vertical, up and down writing

forward slant

Forward-Leaning slant to the right

Now

Very inclined slant

Nope.

Reclined, Left-slanted

LOOKING AT THE SLANT

Writing slant changes all the time but reveals a lot about the emotional nature of the writer. Does yours lean to the left, right, straight up-and-down or in various indifferent directions?

Vertical, Up-and-Down Writing—the United Kingdom's school model—suggests a head over heart emotional attitude (like most cool-headed Brits). You're predictable, mechanical and consistent, but also emotionally passive and inhibited. Resourceful, thoughtful and organized, you tend to do things slowly so that you see what's really happening. You're self-reliant and live in the now. Others may criticize you for being slow, but that may mean that they are not as careful as you are. In everything you do, you want to be able to point to practical, real results.

A Forward-Leaning Slant to the Right (also called "_inclined_") reveals an emotionally healthy individual who is seldom self-demonstrative. Logic and judgement rules. You pay attention to details and protocol. Open-minded, you like to think and plan carefully, and don't jump to conclusions. If you cannot do something well, you are not likely to do it at all.

When Very Inclined, you laugh and cry readily, expressing your feelings impulsively. You have a rich imagination and identify with your surroundings and other's opinions. You may have some difficulty keeping your feelings and intellect from contaminating each other. People feel comfortable in conversation with you. You relate to others with compassion but not pretense. You are deeply sensitive to your environment and friends, and truly want to understand both as fully as possible.

Reclined, Left-Slanting Script suggests emotional withdrawal, being overly aware of other's opinions of you or what you know. Deep within, you long to be different but may hold on to the behavior of your past or your mother's values. Disappointments are common in your life because you suffer with others in their grief or are overly sensitive to

status quo. Your father may have played a weak or negative role in your youth. Learn to accept people at their level of development and don't give them attributes they haven't earned or deserved.

Extremely reclined left-slanting script suggests that the writer lives in the past. Your early conditioning did not prepare you to deal successfully with the circumstances of everyday living and you may have learned to expect the worst. Many view you as difficult to get along with and you tend to keep others at arm's length. You need to be able to confide in someone close to whom you can trust. Emotional fulfillment comes through contact with serious or mature individuals.

Invariable, every which-way, scattered slanted writing suggests an unsettled, inconsistent, mood-swinging kind of person who's emotionally all over the map. You always feel that the answers you get are somehow not final. However, you lack the patience or devotion to stay focused on any one interest for very long. Emotionally, you are cold, although sociable. Slow down!

There are hundreds of other factors to consider for an accurate analysis of writing. For the time being, use the above info with care, compassion and consideration.

I only look like I'm left handed

Extremely reclined, left-slanted

Ain't going there

Invariable slant

HANDWRITING EXERCISE

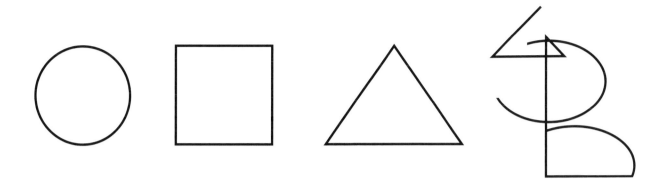

Which of the above geometric forms pleases your eye the most?

These are the dominant symbols of handwriting: circle, square, triangle, and the creative melange of all three. Which prevails in your handwriting?

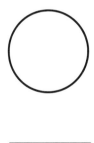

If you chose the **CIRCLE** as your first preference, you are motivated by love, feelings—no sharp edges; like a child's rattle or ball, mother's breasts. The round form frequently appears in the o's, a's, e's, g's, and many upper and lower loops.

When a **SQUARE** is your first selection, you are motivated by a desire for security—like a child's crib or playpen, the walls of your bedroom. The squarish letters include h, m, n, r, p, u, and occasionally, the w.

Your active reserve, integrity, and common sense are divine! You are patient and practical in coping with everyday problems. You always want to be prepared to take advantage of an opportunity that could prove beneficial in the long run.

The **TRIANGLE** as choice number one concerns sex and assertiveness as motivators—normally a child doesn't master this shape until years after scribbling the circle and square. It resembles lightning bolts, knives, church steeples, pine trees and often appears in wedge-like letters such as m, n, r, s, t, w, r and f.

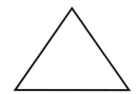

You have strong physical desires and effectively stimulate action. You are fearless in saying what is on your mind, and careless as well. You assert yourself enthusiastically and impulsively.

The **CREATIVE MELANGE** as your first preference says you are motivated by imagination and fantasy—you combine intellect, feelings, logic, energy, and personality (all shapes). Free-form squiggly handwriting often occurs in signatures, embellishments of capital letters, and closing strokes.

You realize your own self-worth, your comprehension is keen. What is obvious to you may be obscure to others. On many subjects, you can speak with authority because you are well informed, always grateful to learn. Your optimism and spirit generates in others a desire to share your excitement as you philosophically "reach for the stars."

CHAPTER TWO

NUMEROLOGY: TIMING IS EVERYTHING

Tell me not in mournful numbers.

—Henry Wadsworth Longfellow

Chances are the sun will rise again tomorrow around the same time. The sunset, ditto. Odds are that you lost your baby teeth about the same age as your mother did, her mom, and even me.

Nine gets you ten that winter will follow autumn this year, one more time.

Cycles.

People, pets, planets, and plants: each have specific unique rhythms that ebb and flow regularly like ocean tides. In numerology, we call them Personal Year cycles. Each of these orderly annual happenings last from one birthday to the next and provide tips about our "new year" shortcomings and successes. There are nine of these ongoing one-year intervals. Personal Numberology Cycles can begin out of sequence, but once they start, they repeat themselves again and again, continually providing tips, options and opportunities to help us (eventually) get "it" right and reap rewards: nine birthday presents 12 months long to enjoy and arm-wrestle with over and over.

After gleaning the personality insights and signals from a client's handwriting sample, I calculate current and upcoming birthday trends. Their handwriting tips me off how they may handle their Personal Numerology's cycles. For example, some people invite change—as revealed from forward right-slanting writing, a harmonious balance in the three Zones, clarity of the script, flowing rhythm—in a Number Nine Personal Year. However, mangled, illegible writing filling the page with baselines falling downwards to the lower right of the page—suggesting depression, weariness—may worry themselves silly during this Year. Mix and match; combine all resources in order to give an accurate assessment. Never judge; only share what you know and offer options on how to cope.

For instance, what you are experiencing now is very similar to the ups and angst nine years ago, eighteen years past, and so on. Personal Year predicting is easy to calculate as well as priceless. Plus, there's no need to understand logarithms, division, or multiplication—only simple addition.

HOW TO FORECAST YOUR COMING YEAR

First: Add the numbers of any year and reduce to a single digit. For example, take a year from the past—1998. Begin by placing plus signs in-between each digit and add them together. Continue to reduce the numbers until you wind up with a single sum total digit. Therefore, 1+9+9+8 adds up to 27; 2+7 reduces to a 9. Taking 2011, a year in the future, this adds up to a 4 (2+0+1+1= 4). This single digit is called a Universal Year.

Secondly: To find your Personal Year, take your birth month and date and add it to any Universal Year. As I'm writing this in 2002, for another example let's play with a March 19th birthday:

    3 (birth month)

  19 (birth date)

2002 (present Universal Year)

2024 = 2+0+2+4 sum total breaks down to 8—so in our example, an EIGHT Personal Year is in effect March 19, 2002 through March 18, 2003; at 2003's birthday, it becomes a NINE Year, in 2004 a ONE Year, and so on. Remember that Personal Years can begin out of sequence but always travel birthday-to-birthday in a merry-go-round circle 1 through 9, then back again to 1 through 9.

Before conducting a Personal Year assessment with your client, ask them to ponder the issues, events, obstacles, joys and delights that they experienced nine years ago. Guess what? It's that time again! And ditto, nine years from now.

THEMES FOR THE ONE PERSONAL YEAR

Over the past 12 months, it was so easy to slide into ruts while the entire world was waiting to be conquered. Well, now it's action time—initiative, independence and leadership is in your stars. The ONE Year speeds self-confidence, courage and frees you from inhibitions. Individual, innovative expression delivers profits and personal perks. At last, you're ready to capitalize on y-o-u. Others may not agree with your actions, but they won't be able to fault your motives. A single-minded approach works best this Year.

Determined, decisive steps win. The ONE Year increases your confidence, helping you make more positive impressions—however, don't rest on laurels. If you feel restricted or encumbered by material possessions, the ONE Year urges you to let go. It's now or never for changes you've been considering. Be they drastic or simple gestures—either will enhance your life. Stand up for your beliefs and others will believe in you. Move forward. Be decisive, act!

Don't be needy for other's approval; you know far more now. Avoid rising to suspicious bait, remain calm. The world is often divided into talkers and doers. Now you're both.

The ONE Year is especially favorable for those born on the 1st, 10th, 19th or 28th of any month.

Keywords & Phrases
- "My way or the highway"
- New beginnings
- Looking out for Number One
- Independence
- "In" with the new
- I can do it!

Shortcomings/Pitfalls
- Arrogance, selfishness
- One-sided love affairs
- Jumping to conclusions; impatience
- Over-optimism
- Short attention span

What to Expect
During the ONE Year, your first duty is to yourself but not at someone else's expense. If you don't fulfill that duty, you'll be little use to anyone. Bark a little louder, push farther and project yourself with more forcefulness than usual. Project ideas with more conviction and get your point across quickly. This is a great Year for getting both feet in new doorways and making a great impression. Pay attention to details and the Big Picture will emerge. Never forget that excuses aren't the same things as reasons.

Going solo brings luck. It's time to mingle, hand out and collect business cards, drop names and "be seen" rather than hide at home or commit to any one group. You have every right to follow your own path. But remember: opening doors is not enough—you must be sure they're the right ones.

You may have difficulty working with others now. Renovate existing relationships so that they embody what you need. You can't make everyone happy. Concentrate on your own well-being. Make judgements for your benefit but don't force your opinions on others without considering other parties and consequences. Beware of compulsive thinking or trying to coerce others by your statements. Feel confident about the direction your life is moving.

What to Avoid

Refuse to let family or friends bully or sway you. It isn't that you're begging for a fight, but you won't easily back down from one, either! Muckraking and name-calling should be avoided this Year. Weigh long-term ventures without shortchanging immediate happiness.

Keep personal affairs squeaky clean because associates from the past are likely to return. Be tolerant of other's views while maintaining your fighting spirit. Often the demands of the outside world become so great that we lose track of what we really need in life and spend time trying to live up to someone else's expectations—don't go there! Admit errors with proud dignity and then go about your merry way.

Don't waste time on small talk. Communication is bottom-line now, so get all the info you need and make the best deal. Your opinion of old associates will change, creating a new set of ground rules.

The past several months have been about closing doors or ending associations that became costly in more ways than one. Put the pieces of your own jigsaw puzzle together and create a glowing new masterpiece of which you can be proud. You're on your way—enjoy it and display yourself to the world!

Tips for Healthier Living During the ONE Year

Improve your health regime and break free from habits that hinder your potential. Try an exercise or weight-loss program, or better eating habits. Seek a thorough health checkup. Now's the time when physicians accurately spot what's been ailing you. Those who normally lack energy or get-up-and-go often "come alive" during the ONE transit because of its energizing effect.

Elective, cosmetic and dental surgery goes well this Year. Schedule corrective procedures, treatments or exams on the 1st, 10th, 19th or 28th of any month.

It's wise to emphasize your eyes this Year. Nearsightedness, astigmatism, cataracts or glaucoma-type problems are likely to surface, so remain alert! High blood pressure, heart palpitations, insomnia, spasms, and irregular breathing may also take center stage.

Soothe jittery nerves and induce restful sleep with a few drops of therapeutic Hops Oil in your bath and sip a relaxing cup of chamomile tea. Burn pink candles for friendship, a rosy remedy for relaxation and a cure to calm jangled nerves.

Ruby is the Personal Year ONE gemstone, long-associated with strengthening the heart and increasing passion. Display it on your altar, dashboard of the car, jewelry.

Emotions, Love & Romance

At this time, predicaments stem from discovering more about yourself and your emotional needs but feeling unable to convey what you have gleaned. However, it could be that you have outgrown certain romantic involvements. This Year, you need more freedom, new challenges and opportunities to paint on a bigger canvas.

During the ONE cycle, you attract people who appreciate your individuality and acknowledge your convictions. However, romance may be awkward or ambivalent because of your newfound desire to spend time alone. The message is clear: the really bad times are over, and no one can restrict or deceive you. Bounce, don't dwell on unhappy or unfortunate experiences. In spite of others' demands, criticisms or disapproval, you must remain in control and keep your hand firmly on the steering wheel—don't settle in the back-seat. And, relationship-wise: don't settle for second-best.

You demand a great deal of yourself and need friends and family who support your high expectations. Offer help and encouragement when necessary but don't display disappointment if they fail to live up to your hopes. With almost everyone on your side, take advantage of advice.

Finances

No matter how frustrated you've been, you're heading back on top this Year. You're far better placed than you seem to appreciate, so accentuate the positive and the negatives will seem less significant. Last Year's numerical nuances pulled you in dozens of directions, so it's important that you follow your instincts and intellect. Don't be afraid to speak your mind—others will.

Although the ONE Year is wonderful for acquiring large ticket items, be on guard about financially overextending yourself or mismanaging monies. Re-examine your relationship with material "things." Do they serve your needs, or are you merely their slave? If you're risk-taking, self-indulgent type, you'll hunger for more and more. Examine extravagance. High-rolling gambling speculations don't fare well now because you're tempted to spend, spend, spend.

However, it's an excellent Year for changing jobs, careers and increasing income. Put business plans into effect and cultivate new contacts now. Talk with supervisors, discuss promotions and game plans

during the 3rd and 9th months following your last birthday. Focused approaches reap dividends.

Confidence in your ideas and beliefs help you take advantage of the many opportunities that come your way this Year. Don't be reluctant to use them. Patience is hardly your strong point now, so keep a cautious rein on your tongue and temper—play for time and you'll play for keeps! Be proud of your accomplishments. Your determination to improve your circumstances means the grass frequently looks greener elsewhere. This Year, however, you should have no trouble ensuring that your lawn is the finest in the neighborhood.

Using your ONE Year to the Fullest

Examine last birthday's problems. You have it in your power to outrun and upstage opposition now, but unless you maintain complete confidence in yourself, you will be unable to do so. Long-term assets count more than transient pleasures now.

Legal, business and professional matters run smoother this Year. Recognition from recent efforts and relationships with authority figures excel. Don't exaggerate the importance of a difference of opinion: it matters less than you think. Believe, and make real. Knowing what you want is important. Working harder than your norm is common. You have more going for you than you may realize. Have faith and take care of yourself.

Take the lead and don't hide in the corner nor settle for second-place. Over the coming months, you're more ready, willing and able to fight for your rights. Demonstrate to the world what you're capable of doing. Make a concerted effort to transform your anxieties, then renew your efforts. Time invested now brings dividends.

Be positive! You're heading in the right direction.

Author Dr. Kevin Leman claims that you are perfectionistic, reliable, conscientious, and well-organized if you are the first born in a family—similar to what you experience throughout a Personal Year Number One (regardless of your birth order). If you are the baby in the family, Leman claims that you are manipulative, blame others and are precocious—just like everybody feels during Year Nine. Like the flow of Personal Years, as important as a child's order of birth may be, it is only an influence, not a concrete fact.

THEMES FOR THE TWO PERSONAL YEAR

Face it: last birthday was challenging because you had to deal with matters on your own. But now, your nearest and dearest, home and partnerships take the spotlight. It's time to search inside yourself, find comfort with your feelings and moods, change decor or dwellings and, maybe even relationships!

You may feel less self-reliant than usual, for it's a cycle when interaction with others is more likely than going solo. Mutual trust is all-important, so be frank, play fair and be discriminating.

Dealings with women are more profound now. Love relationships throughout this number-transit signifies deep emotional experiences that can be either positive or negative. Whether love or money, be careful about games in which you and lady friends manipulate emotions to gain power over each other. Be alert to feelings of possessiveness and jealousy.

Compromise, don't cringe. "Attract" rather than "aggravate."

Whatever seeds you planted during your last birthday are now in the germination stage. Changes are likely to be slow and gradual rather than rapid or intense like last year's ONE Year. The tip for the TWO Year is to establish and maintain a peaceful, mellow balance.

Keywords & Phrases
- Companionship
- Patience
- Teamwork
- Tact
- Peace-making
- Sentimentality

Shortcomings/Pitfalls
- Prejudice
- Nagging
- Over-sensitivity
- Exaggeration
- Pettiness
- Melancholy
- Apathy

What to Expect
"Stuff" concerning mother, sister, wife, daughter, nieces, aunts or grandmothers is on the increase. While you are more aware of your feelings now, don't let them overwhelm you. There is nothing wrong with criticism as long as it's constructive and well-intended. This Year, flexibility is your most valuable asset. Even discordant contact with loved ones is likely to do more good than harm.

Naturally, there will be delays and hindrances as well as setbacks. Practice patience and perseverance and apply elbow grease slowly yet steadily. The more solid the foundation of projects/hopes/dreams, the more successfully they will manifest.

Your attention will turn to philosophy, religion or other subjects that encompass life as a whole on an intellectual, lofty and spiritual level. Now more than ever, your artistic muse gets aroused and the desire for comfort and beauty takes center stage.

Others will feel compelled to express problems they have with you, so don't expect to enjoy everything you hear. This is a time when tensions must be quickly released, possibly by either renovating y-o-u or relocating h-o-m-e.

The TWO transit leans toward extravagance or overindulgence for things that feel, taste and look good. Question passing fancies and stay on your toes. With the right attitude you can turn dreams into reality now. Keep an eye on your credit card balance and postpone power shopping until another birthday!

What to Avoid

Don't play martyr! Trickery or deception is likely throughout the 1st, 5th and 9th months following your birthday. Old habits, prejudices or childhood patterns may overwhelm what you usually consider reasonable because you crave emotional reassurance from familiar objects, people and places. Be careful about being around negative people who are not willing to discuss things rationally.

You're likely to feel attracted to someone weaker than you who needs nurturing and protection. Confrontations with women, both positive and negative, are passionate and heated. Beware of reacting automatically or according to habit. Old points of view are likely to mislead.

View all TWO tensions as opportunities to see parts of yourself that need improving. You may have feelings of inferiority or guilt, usually for no reason. Thus, you may get easily discouraged by circumstances and withdraw into your own private world, causing you to miss opportunity and happiness. Wise, heart-felt communication is just what the digit-doctor orders.

Tips for Healthier Living During the TWO Year

Aim for "healthy mind, healthy body." Physically at this time, the kidneys are especially vulnerable, as well as disorders that result from emotional stress such as ulcers, stomach or gastric problems. TWO Year women may experience more than the average female problems, as well. Don't force yourself into doing something you really don't have the energy to do. Loud voices and high-decibel music will take its toll on your nerves, disposition and digestion now.

Avoid the use of drugs or alcohol, because they may reinforce or increase unwelcome emotions of

clinging or withdrawal from reality, which will further cloud the real issues of your life. Allergic reactions to foods and beverages are also likely at this number-time, which is another reason to be careful about what you consume.

Bathe in a few drops of therapeutic lavender oil to soothe jangled nerves. Your lucky, centering colors are shades of turquoise and purple. For meditation and calmness, burn white, baby blue, or violet candles.

The multi-hued agate is the Personal Year Number TWO gemstone. Used by the Magi of ancient Persia for averting tempests, it was also helpful in promoting the growth of crops. It has been reported to possess high medicinal value as an antidote for physical and mental ailments that result from exhaustion and is said to insure long life, joy, and eloquence.

Emotions, Love & Romance

You're finally able to express affection more easily and make your feelings more clear to your partner. It's a fun and flirty year—and, for some, a time when a wholly new love may enter your life. Readily express your love and affection as others will respond genuinely. For lovers, this is an extremely amorous time as you feel a real need and desire to give and receive love. Aim for a conscious understanding of what you expect from each other.

In friendships, you may be attracted to younger folks who make you happy without too many strings attached. Enjoy their counsel because they are likely to be a great help. Don't waste the day (or night) by yourself! Under this transit, love is not an intellectual abstraction; it is something felt and expressed through emotions and body. If you normally have trouble talking about your feelings for others, this year you will be more articulate and confident. It's an excellent Year for entertaining at home—especially small groups. The TWO Year delivers grace, ease and pleasant loving interaction into your life. Keep your options open and your faith intact. Move forward, and begin afresh.

Finances

This is a good Year for collecting debts from the past. Unexpected opportunities from peers come swiftly. Be receptive to the ideas of others and enjoy improved relationships with superiors. Now more than ever, you are willing to work with others to resolve difficulties and improve interpersonal relationships. At this time, you are able to combine breadth of vision with intuition with sharp perception and thereby see a new scope of your money-making abilities.

Be careful not to let your amiability with coworkers prevent you from standing up for your own rights. Don't worry about alienating fellow employees or peers because now you are able to make it clear that you are working for everyone's mutual benefit.

It is sometimes possible to travel further in your head and heart than by more conventional means. Under the TWO influence, you should have no shortage of brilliant ideas.

Best day for job interviewing or seeking a promotion is Tuesday (Two's Day).

How to use the TWO Year to your fullest advantage

This is the Year for dealing with domestic, personal and emotional matters—milk it to the max! Relationships are usually quite good and rewarding now, and those that you have been building up for years may begin to produce results, however fleeting. Now, others sense the sincerity of your feelings more and will respond in kind. Think realistically as well because it may be difficult making logical decisions. Redefine your relationship with women closest to you.

You will feel protective and more nurturing of loved ones, wanting to help in any way. This is an ideal time for doing charitable or community work, for talking with your minister or rabbi, working with hobbies and showing special kindness to friends or family who may feel forgotten. Harmony and cooperation are paramount.

Long distance travel and overseas voyages get the thumbs up now. Additional TWO Year perks include letter-writing, journal-keeping, publishing and luck from e-mail. Your opinions flow with less resistance, and life seems to be easier now. As a consequence, you can relate to people more easily, for others perceive your inward harmony and are drawn to you because of it. Old, tried and true friends are rewarding now.

Any headway you make now will ease your path in the future. Others may not agree with your actions, but they should not be able to fault your motives! Don't get aggravated over a lost opportunity or unrecognized talent. This Year, your confidence will return and you'll be able to demonstrate your competence. By the middle of your next birthday, you'll forget what all the fuss was about.

THEMES FOR THE THREE PERSONAL YEAR

Need a new job? The THREE Year is the time to begin plugging' away, laying the groundwork and getting ready for a new paycheck (shortly down the pike)! This Year, you'll clear away many fruitless limitations, whether imposed by yourself or others. It's time for being playful, expanding your circle of friends and gearing up for better business.

Because you're anxious to soothe ruffled feelings and not say anything unpleasant, you're finally ready to smooth over any rough edges that may have cropped up recently in relationships. You won't be as shy or worry as much as last year when you finally encounter new people, nor will you find yourself fretting about making a bad impression. By playing your cards right, this will be a very helpful Year for contractual negotiations, conferences, planning sessions, discussions. However, the keyword is "contacts," not "cash." So update your resume and paperwork now!

Communicate confidentially with new individuals. Write. Experiment with a course of action for your career or personal life—or both! Making plans rather than manifesting pesos is your favored fuel this Year. You're more intellectually alive now, curious, and willing to learn and earn. Those who challenge your thinking or ideas will not bother you as they may have done before.

Because you have something to say and nothing to hide, public appearances excel. But beware not to overextend yourself. Plan, restrain. Luck will not bring success—only elbow grease, insight, skill and connections. You now have more initiative than usual, and you can accomplish a great deal.

Spurn the dull, boring and humdrum this Year. You're going to want to move forward now, and experience anything and everything! Make a conscious concerned effort to communicate about matters that are important to you. Your ability to keep track of details, rather than the larger picture, rules.

This is a favorable Year for keeping an open eye for "the next things," travelling, pleasure, brainstorming and much laughter. Philosophy, religion and literary concerns will be the center of much discussion. Dream about what you want, luxuries and comfort comes soon.

Keywords & Phrases
- Activity
- Self-improvement
- Short trips
- New friends, associates
- Promoting your word
- Improved luck

Shortcomings/Pitfalls

- Pulled in too many directions
- Overspending
- Jealousy, suspicion
- Spreading yourself too thin
- Drifting without purpose
- Overly concerned about what others think and do; gossip

What to Expect

A quick and fast-paced twelve months is ahead! The THREE Year attracts opportunity, pleasure and popularity. Circumstances will arise that give you increased freedom or an opportunity to do something that you have never done before. Your newfound ability to see the larger view enables you to plan with foresight. Where others see only confusion, you'll see clarity (or options, at least). Seek advancement, achievement, recognition, approval and appreciation, now. It's finally easier to act with more freedom, less restraints, even though you may not be very tolerant of red tape.

Ridding yourself from past debts and diminishing your losses are in the stars. Seeds planted a little over two years ago soon bear fruit. Provided that you are careful not to overdo it, this is an excellent Year to expand your investments. However, beware that there's a larger degree of impulsiveness this Year or a tendency to leap to conclusions. Plan, don't plummet.

Education is a-okay; travel (for future business) is terrific. Keeps your mind occupied. Now is a good time for artistic activity, as well as getting together with others for creative, artistic purposes. It's better to work *with* others rather than be the leader.

Be careful not to get so carried away by enthusiasm and self-expression that your thinking or work gets sloppy. Your hopes and wishes are very important, now...but don't neglect the reality of day-to-day needs. Because new or radical ideas will bother you less than normal, the THREE Year finds you more eager than usual. You're more fascinated by fantasies because they broaden your understanding of the world around you. But can you afford them NOW? Smile and simmer before signing any dotted line.

The idea of traveling to foreign places is especially appealing during a THREE Year. Whenever at all possible, break with your usual routine and attempt to go somewhere. If time or money is limited, experiment shopping at different malls or communities that you usually do not frequent. The break will do you good. (Remember to bring your biz cards!)

What to Avoid

During the THREE Year, there's a tendency to scatter yourself and not think clearly or carefully. The danger of making decisions impulsively without adequate forethought or being easily swayed by others gets exaggerated. So, watch your step! Be careful not to get carried away by enthusiasm that your thinking becomes sloppy. And don't fall victim to the delusion that you cannot be wrong about anything.

Don't let your financial affairs get out of hand, now. This Year, you're a dreamer and schemer... not a doer, especially. You may get overcommitted to projects that demand more time and money than you really have. Don't overestimate your resources! Make sure that you are in a position to change your mind (which you will do with great regularity) in order to prevent frustration.

You'll probably discover that some point of view you have held is not correct any which way. A person whom you had a definite opinion of, either positive or negative, may be quite different from what you thought. As you expand your own spheres of interest, influence and experience, don't overtax your own strength, psychologically or physically. If you're inclined to indulge in such risks as gambling or speculative financial ventures, understand that it is not actually "luck" that brings the rewards, but your confidence that makes you a winner.

Your natural curiosity is at a peak now. However, you may not be very disciplined, so you must be very strong. Due to the abundant energy the THREE Year delivers, you're not as tolerant to the "boredom" of studying, cramming for exams, or test taking. Although you may not be consciously aware of it, everything you say is conditioned by the habits and patterns of last Year and ingrained from childhood. Now it may come out as an inappropriate message, one that doesn't apply to the moment-at-hand.

Test your beliefs and make sure that they stand up to rigorous analysis. Don't be afraid to experiment with new ideas, but don't accept them uncritically either. Rely more on your inner senses and feelings. Clear thinking is not this Year's strong point; only enthusiasm to move forward, be free.

**Tips for Healthier Living
During the THREE Year**

An irritated or frequent sore throat, vocal infections, problems with the liver and assorted skin disorders are known to flare up during a THREE Year. Now is a good time to avoid stimulants and unhealthy foods. Exhaustion from nerves, insomnia is common. Stress factors may be on the rise and disorders that stem from anxiety may increase. Stay especially alert to health matters during the 1st, 3rd, 5th and 10th month following your birthday.

Due to the fast pace of the THREE Year (or absent-mindedness), avoid the use of alcohol or drugs because overdoing comes easy. Allergic reactions to food or beverages are likely at this time. Take advantage of your increased vigor and involve yourself in sports, yoga or bodybuilding. Since this Year favors group involvment, join a health club. Establish your individuality through learning and/or working with others.

Bathe in a few drops of therapeutic rosemary oil to soothe tension and fatigue. Burn gold candles to promote well being and attract prosperity. THREE Year's health-giving colors are ivory, pink and cobalt blue.

The aquamarine is your gemstone now. The ancient Romans believed that this gem bestowed good spirits on its wearers and heals throat, stomach and liver ailments. It is associated with wisdom and musical talent and is said to enhance lover's communication.

Emotions, Love & Romance

The THREE Year stimulates personal freedom. The more you feel that anyone is holding you back, the more you will resist. This is especially true in personal relationships. If your partner becomes possessive or limits your freedom, you will resist and fight louder than the year before. Plus, you now desire a life away from the home—dine out, do theater, take a stroll. Last Year was "stay in." This Year is "get me outta here." (That won't last long, trust me.)

It's easy in the THREE Year to become totally possessed by newly discovered beliefs and convictions and insist on forcing them on others—so watch out. You may also become so obsessed with working out an idea—or, work—which may be perfectly valid, that you can't get any peace until you have done so. This could lead to a nervous condition or breakdown. Don't overstrain. Restrain!

Don't act impulsively. While you will feel an urge to assert yourself this Year, don't overdo it. It is common during a THREE-transit to experience emotional unrest that is likely to disturb your own peace of mind as well as your relations, especially those who make emotional demands.

Be receptive and attentive. This is not a time to tell "just anyone" about your private "stuff." Listen carefully. Examine others' points of view and try to find a common ground of cooperation. You may feel overly generous and not exercise proper restraint with confidential matters best not discussed.

Rise above confusion, doubt, or uncertainty. Let matters be. Wait for situations to settle down. You're likely to have feelings that, by yourself, you are not quite complete and that you need someone else to make you "whole." You do not have to search for True Affection. The time has come to let others know that you are capable of standing on your own two feet. Let it be. Enjoy what is around you every day.

Finances

The THREE Year is good for business leads but not cash flow or investments. Sorry. Beware of overextending (financially as well as socially).

However, the THREE Year is a good time for selling items, trimming down—but not for large investments. Garage or estate sales get the thumbs up now.

Your intellectual curiosity is stronger in the THREE Year, making this is a good time for business seminars, conferences.

Wednesdays bring you luck throughout the THREE Year. Best times for advancement, promotion are the 3rd, 6th and 9th months following your last birthday. The enthusiasm, buoyancy and optimism associated with this number-transit makes you

noticed by those who count. Your home life may take second place to your professional life, so don't plan on too much 'listening ear' domestic-time.

Job interviewing goes well , although erratic, now. Follow up on resumes, telephone calls to improve your good fortune. Keep others informed of your whereabouts. Go to parties, open houses and fund-raisers. Meet people whom you've admired for a long while, or who could get your ideas or income off the ground. Late summer of your THREE Year begets best bets for the buck.

Let everyone else know that you are an original. Dress differently. Feng Shui or redecorate your office. Do everything that sets you apart. In the THREE Year, it is your exceptional personality that brings you the breaks—so capitalize on it! Don't kowtow or crumble!

How to Use the THREE Year to Your Fullest Advantage

No doubt you have been provoked beyond endurance and now feel the need to distance yourself from those that make you feel insecure. Because the THREE Year is a "getaway-from-what-ails-me" time, you must remember that old habits of three years ago certainly will continue to repeat themselves until you realize you don't have to tolerate these slights!

Be more awake and alive, mentally and socially and economically—get out of the comfort zone. This is an excellent year for attracting support to help you

tackle problems that you've been unable to solve with tried and true convictions. You can appreciate that every journey of a thousand miles begins with a single step—so get going and make sure that those in positions of power recognize your worth!

Talk with others, even about matters that you usually find difficult to discuss. Negotiate and share the feelings that you became more aware of throughout your TWO Year. Communications flow more

> **Many people experience a change of residency or others when they are leaving home base during the Personal Years Three and Six—think "new faces, new places."**

smoothly and are less emotional now: let others really hear your two-cents' worth.

The gulf between what you'd like to do and what your resources will permit is getting wider, but you are soon approaching a windfall. Get on the circuit and, at the same time, work out how to reduce your overhead. Could it also be the case that you've become too financially dependent on another individual?

THEMES FOR THE FOUR PERSONAL YEAR

Why dwell on frenzy when the future is so promising? Don't let yourself be dissuaded from your intended course of action. "Fine print" begets "financial rewards" now. However, the tempo of the FOUR Year is conservative, slow-mo. FOUR favors tradition over anything new, for the sake of novelty or status quo. The FOUR provides an escape route, but it is up to you to finalize details and read the small print. You are the best judge of your capabilities this Year. Once committed, nothing will stop you!

You are finally in a position to make things go your way, financially. Whatever your age or circumstances, the time has come to listen to your head rather than your heart. No one has the right to tell you how to live. You are in a position to make the rules: do so! You have never been better placed to achieve success or recognition. If others show disapproval, that's their problem. Something learned from a surprising source should work in your favor so long as you understand its true value and implications. Be ready to act. You have demonstrated patience; the wait will be worthwhile.

Make your life more secure. If your expectations are overly optimistic, you may be disappointed, but at least the reasons will become more clear in the coming months. This Year is one for cutting back and seeking stable foundations. Expansion? Yes. Growth? Indeed! In fact, too much emphasis on the past may be the reason for what has hindered your progress.

Organize before exploring. Outline, plot, and look ahead without expectation but with positive enthusiasm. Behave yourself, watch what you say and do.

You may surprise yourself how carefully you handle money and esteem, now, as it a badge of success rather than as a medium for extravagance. If you feel that you've been cheated recently, don't make mountains out of molehills. Put your life in order! Adverse activity from last Year may be making you feel more like the sacrificial lamb rather than the sprightly mountain goat. However, what transpires over the coming months should enable you to sever unprofitable ties, discard what is false or harmful while laying groundwork for a more secure, comfortable existence.

Self-discipline delivers rewards. It's time to work, tend to business matters, face reality. More will be required of you; make time to build upwards. Change employers, careers and get the economic ball in motion! The pleasure of work is enjoying "work." You simply cannot afford to devote so much time to propping up other's egos.

Keywords & Phrases

- New financial foundations
- Reputation
- Organization
- Focus
- Tradition over novelty
- Slow and steady

Shortcomings/Pitfalls

- Neglecting responsibility
- Spending more, earning less
- Escapism, complaining
- Discouragement; cheating
- Dogmatic

What to Expect

You're able to work more patiently and improve long-range goals while dealing with everyday concerns. Talk to superiors about your job, your needs, your intentions and how you may advance. This is an excellent Year for examining your hopes and ideals, and evaluate how well they have served you. Now, your critical faculty is extremely sharp, and you can see flaws in other's arguments more objectively.

This is a "reaping rewards time" filled with intense sessions of detail-tending or unglamorous routine. Enjoy it as you enlarge your scope of activity. Go places and do things you haven't done before. You work best by yourself this Year because you're more conscious of the larger scheme. Finally, it's easier to manage yourself rather than others. View any conflict as homework, for it is certainly not intended to defeat you—only help you graduate into the next exciting stage of your development. You are on the way up again! Be sure you know the true value of what you discard.

Everything you do now is rewarded due to foresight, planning and understanding essentials that make projects successful. But if you don't take the initiative, your FOUR won't be powerful enough by itself to drive you forward.

What to Avoid

Follow-through with what is already underway. Finish what is incomplete and simplify. Old tasks that have not been completed must be tied up and concluded now. Unfortunately, layoffs, shut-downs, or strikes are likely now. Roll with all punches. It may be difficult to keep the real and the ideal sorted out. Refuse to get wrapped in abstract speculations or high ideals that are impossible to actualize.

You may feel that the world "owes" you something, whether or not you deserve it. It may also make you feel as though others should be breaking their backs trying to help you. Your superiors may give you more responsibility than you choose to have. This may not be an easy-going or light-hearted time, but works to your advantage. Don't get discouraged. Instead, cut your losses and disengage yourself from activities that create difficulties. Act now; play to win.

Above all, watch your health this Year! Sloppiness in any department, whether physical, mental, spiritual or intellectual, must not be tolerated.

Because of the pressure of circumstances and the need to get things done, you may have less free time. It may not be an especially light-hearted Year, but you will be productive! Delegate and do!

Tips for Healthier Living
During the FOUR Year

The teeth, bones, urinary, and circulatory systems are especially vulnerable during a FOUR Year, as well as risks to the arms and feet. Proper diet and eating/meditation habits are important now. Be wise and exercise. Your energy level is high and you are able to accomplish a lot of work in a short time. Be alert when driving and avoid speeding. Avoid excessive physical strain because your body is more subject than usual to minor infections, chills, or fever.

Changes in moods and general health are likely to occur during the 4th, 8th, and 12th months following your birthday.

To feel revitalized and refreshed this Year, take a therapeutic bath with a few drops of pine oil. Burn orange candles for focus and meditation.

Allergies are likely to increase. Your body is especially sensitive to drugs now so double-check all medical prescriptions. Treat yourself to a massage as often as possible. If you don't find a satisfactory outlet to work off everyday tension, you may find yourself easily angered and quick to take offense.

The FOUR Year gemstone is the garnet, long-associated with statesmen and authority figures. It's said to promote success in business and victory in competitive endeavors. Legend proclaims that it encourages good disposition and faithful affections. It also has a dramatic reputation for protecting wearers against poison, lightning, and shipwrecks!

Emotions, Love & Romance

This Year's spotlight is on the "serious" as opposed to life's lighter side, making it a terrific time for establishing and furthering friendships as well as family relations.

Generally, relationships and marriage in a FOUR Year are long lasting, good investments. However, arguments, obstinacy, and stubbornness may prevail. Now's the time to detach from petty concerns and look at the over all picture of your life's desires. Allow loved ones the same freedom. You may become overbearing or demanding without offering anything to your partner in return, unwilling to wait for others to make the first move.

Be open to others' points of view. Your mind is extremely sharp this Year. You are very conscious of flaws, the unhappy or indifferent aspects of life and may overlook the true meaning of unity. Divorce this Year will be rather unpleasant.

However, the FOUR begets balance for your emotional needs and better understanding about duty

and obligation. Pay attention to what you're told. Don't rush into matters; confidence and experience are the products of patience and hard work. Know the value of what you discard.

Finances

This is a good time for buying, selling, trading, and activities concerned with building your future. Set up a budget and stick to it. Overall, the FOUR Year is a good for lawsuits, marketing last Year's products and cleaning out useless inventory. This is a good Year for investors, art dealers and those in the fields of engineering and mechanical technology.

Leases signed during the Number FOUR Year will hold you to fine print. This is a good time for dealing with realtors, property development, resort investments and negotiating with landlords.

Although your mind is earthbound this year, you will not lack vision or foresight. Therefore, it is an excellent time to expand an existing business. After you find the most practical solution to any problem, move immediately in that direction. New offers may provide improved opportunities for getting ahead.

If you are in business for yourself: expand! Dare to do more than you have ever done before, but balance your daring with reason and care. Don't compromise what you know is right for you.

How to use the FOUR Year to Your Fullest

Square up past mistakes and avoid making new ones. You've withheld your opinion long enough, so speak up! Don't let past events thwart your ability to cope with the present.

Order, management, purpose, de-cluttering and living sanely are keynotes now.

Whatever happens, the end result is that your way of making a living becomes a source of excitement and positive challenge. Don't get upset by change; establish new roots. If you don't make the effort to construct a solid base now, you will have difficulty later when your concerns turn elsewhere. The feeling of belonging is strong now.

When your career or business expands, apply gains to your personal life and invest. Think personal growth! Don't be hasty. Be a better human being, as well as breadwinner.

Perseverance wins out, wishing won't. Don't waste the Year dreaming how you are going to spend a windfall.

THEMES FOR THE FIVE PERSONAL YEAR

The tempo is brisk and you're ready to take risks. However, you are also inclined to be sloppy, so double-check everything you do. There's a need to restore balance this Year. It is essential that you recognize your true priorities. Before giving in to others, you must decide whether what you're hearing is to your advantage.

Lately, you may have been trying to do too much, running the risk of undermining everything you have achieved thus far. A change of scenery or circumstances is the answer this Year, but only if you relax and stop worrying about what you should be doing.

The need for acknowledgement may become more exaggerated this Year. This is a time of vigorous self-assertion because your mind is more alert, sharp. It's now time to take initiative and begin new projects because you have the drive and energy for follow through. Tackle unresolved problems. Don't waste the next twelve months doing same old, same old routine. Working alone or in seclusion is favored. Without being excessively aggressive, you will make it crystal-clear to associates that you are willing to work for what you want. You can't succeed at everything—you have to decide which parts of your life require special attention.

This is an important Year especially if you were born on the 5th, 14th or 23rd of any month.

Personal magnetism and sex appeal (as well as pregnancy) is at an all time high now. By and large, the emphasis is on warm bodies rather than deep emotional companionship. Don't be pressured into going against your beliefs.

Keywords & Phrases
- Time to be seen and heard
- Stand up for your rights
- Inner fortitude and strength
- Variety and change
- The FIVE senses of the body
- Health & sex issues

Shortcomings/Pitfalls
- Jumping to conclusions; pushy
- Scattered energy; unfocused
- Over-eating, over-indulgence; insomnia
- Impulsiveness; false accusations
- Self-righteousness
- Fear; imagined illnesses/weakness

What to Expect
The FIVE Year is fast-paced, bringing new contacts and opportunities for growth, expansion. "Restlessness" is your shortcoming. You will feel uncertainty,

confusion; matters seem to need immediate action rather than contemplation. You're not satisfied with daily routine now.

Focus on yourself, where you are heading and want to go. Plan intelligently and work with wisdom rather than impulse. Efforts to liberate yourself from unnecessary or inhibiting restrictions bring success. But beware of power struggles and ego conflicts. Convince others that your mutual interests are interdependent.

The FIVE Year favors working alone because you may not think in "group" terms. Whatever you do, make sure that you have plenty of room to move. You have the ability to make penetrating analyses about human nature, but be careful to edit what you say.

Therefore, you may spend more money than you can afford. You can chip away at a financial problem for only so long before it must be tackled head-on. With no shortage of ideas about how to resolve issues, you need to identify those with potential and those that are unrealistic. Patience and understanding gets you where you want to go.

This cycle is concerned about how you present yourself in the face of pressure around your home and work. Stay strong! Refrain from being domineered by others. You are filled with energies that want to cry to the world: "I am!" What seemed impossible last year will become plausible.

What to Avoid

Keep arrogance and ego in check as pride needs constant control. Know when to be still and when to listen. It's time to impress others—just don't beat anybody over the head with your opinions. You know you'll get where you're going—it's just a matter of time.

Since you are likely to find yourself doing too much at once this Year, avoid anything that makes you frantic. Work with time, your schedule, limitations. Don't get involved in so many projects that you can't devote adequate thought to any one.

Be willing to work with other people. Think in terms of mutual growth rather than selfish ends. This is a danger time for alienating people through self-righteousness.

Quickly concluded projects are favored over long-term ones. Home-wise, the fewer radical changes made, the better. Domestic strife is another side of this transit that you may confront. Make an effort to agree with those whom you live with and try to see their side. Be wary of new relationship formed in your FIVE Year because you may lack discrimination. Remember that although everything has its price, at times that price is too high.

Tips for Healthier Living During the FIVE Year

Because energy levels are high this Year, take time to relax and visit the doctor; you may not realize how

hard your body and mind are working, so there is a real danger that you will overwork, over-do, be more accident-prone or take foolish risks because you assume that nothing is wrong. Don't overindulge in rich food or drink. Moderation is extremely important. Guard health especially during the 1st, 4th, 8th and 10th months after your birthday.

This Year's health-giving colors to wear are shades of green and red. Burn green candles to help channel energy and passion.

The sapphire, ancient symbol of wisdom, is the gemstone throughout your FIVE Personal Year. It is said to be a potent love talisman for arousing love and faithfulness in marriage/unions. Wear one on a necklace, ring, bracelet or display on a bedroom altar. The sapphire is known for its healing qualities, as well as being a powerful aid for peace of mind and fulfilling prayers.

Emotions, Love & Romance

Personal contact with others dominates the FIVE Year. However, you may yearn to be involved in a "relationship" so much at this time, that you wind up not caring whether or not it goes smoothly. You are

far less tolerant with others' quirks and may find people's peculiarities irritating now. In all close relationships, there is compromise, real complaints are shelved, which in the long run weakens even the best unions. Now is the time when repressed grievances should be brought into the open, which can result in a concise, exhilarating clearing of the air.

You may feel a strong conflict between what you think of yourself and what or where you think you should be now. Don't fall into negative thinking or downgrade yourself. Will what you stand to gain make up for what you lose?

On the other side of the coin, there's a tendency to flatter yourself that you are the most fascinating and interesting person in the world. If you are not given this recognition, you are likely to become angry and more easily involved in disputes. Be careful that confidence doesn't translate into arrogance.

Finances

Guard finances carefully as you will attract and dream up many "get rich quick" schemes. Now is the time to promote and advertise yourself, but don't buy on spec. Another trait of the FIVE Year is one of reversals: good to bad, bad to good. For example, a failing business will usually bankrupt under this cycle. Although this may sound negative, what transpires will frees you to explore positive, lucrative avenues.

During the FIVE Year, thinking often becomes overwhelmed by detailed matters that seem impor-tant at the moment but wind up being of little significance. "Thinking small" is a problem.

Push for more responsibilities at work during the 3rd month following your birthday. This is your best time for talking to superiors, asking for a raise, seek new employment. Your attitude about money is changing now, so demand a clear explanation and second opinion.

Using the FIVE Year to Your Fullest Advantage

Inner strength and determination rules. No matter how sensitive or vulnerable you feel, it would be a mistake to take every comment to heart. With confidence and fortitude, you will be victorious. Luck comes from older people or professionals who offer support, answers. Common sense and stick-to-itive-ness—rather than intuition or gut-feelings—wins.

Personal pushes for success may arouse opposition, so be careful about breaking any rules of the "game." Your concept of yourself and goals are changing, making you a new and improved person. Be satisfied with the rewards of the day. Whatever you do, you will better understand and drive forward with vigor.

Others may try to play on your weaknesses, but the fact is that you are considerably stronger than they—and possibly you—appreciate. So much has changed in recent years and, inevitably, you have changed with it. No one is trying to block your progress; it's just that others need to know exactly what to do.

THEMES FOR THE SIX PERSONAL YEAR

The SIX Year favors romance, courtship and domesticity. You have seldom been better positioned to make your mark on a person or place. In fact, there is little you will not achieve over the next Year—provided you set your mind and heart to it. This is a good time to make peace with your enemies, redefine partnerships, renovate homebase.

"Unions" are emphasized throughout the SIX Year. Marriage or vows of commitment are likely as well as lucky. Relations with parents improve. But remember that love and hate are two sides of the same coin, and it's easy to mistake one for the other when emotions run high. If someone tries to push you to extremes this Year, understand all subtext before you act—or react. It's a terrific time for experimenting with your hairdresser for a new look, re-doing your dwelling, and/or other things that make you feel comfortable and good.

You'll want to help your friends in every way and will feel more protective, nurturing. If you work with others, you're able to keep things running smoothly now because of an increased understanding about their feelings. But there are some problems: if you are jealous or possessive, it will produce feelings of affection that suffocate. Recognize that even the closest relationship needs room to breathe. Avoid being overprotective.

Let others know you care; don't leave it up to imagination. Make sure that everyone is on the same page or you will end up weeping or wasting your time.

Keywords & Phrases
- Family; dealings with old friends
- Love/sex relations
- The arts
- Home
- Joyful, social activity

Shortcomings/Pitfalls
- Whining; brooding
- Self-righteous; fault-finding
- Unfair; prejudiced
- Isolation
- Clannish; jealous

What to Expect
Many SIX Year rewards are spiritual or emotional, not financial. Be sure everyone is working together and on the same wavelength. Rifts between lovers or friends are patched up quicker now. Don't make excuses. Emphasize enjoyment!

The SIX Year relates to the theatre and arts, the harmonious and beautiful. Psychologically, you're more in

sync with "balance." Energies flow with less resistance and the pace of your life becomes easier, mellower. As a result, you find yourself relating to people with more ease. Doubts about the recent past are inevitable, but that is no reason to lower your sights or lose your sense of purpose. You're more sensitive to other's feelings now, and better understand how to constructively use those energies for positive needs.

Female friends or relatives that you've shared past experiences become more important now. Talk over old times and engage in sentimental reverie. Then again, you may feel like doing nothing more exciting than staying home with the VCR or curling up with a good book. Be careful not to become too passive. There is a tendency throughout the SIX to expect others to cater to you, do errands or expect "circumstances" to take care of you.

What to Avoid

Don't become possessive or petty. Beware of gossiping about others, scandal and legal matters that you know are shaky or not above-board. You may feel unappreciative and misunderstand other's assistance. Share your doubts.

Don't let shadows of the past prevent you from living in the present or plan for the future—especially now when the outlook is so promising! Drop unconstructive traits. Don't waste time worrying. You're undergoing many changes of heart—don't fight it! Resist the desire to use subversive tactics to control, since that will create bitterness, which could ultimately destroy whatever bond or goodwill exists.

You may find it difficult to give in or compromise either in love or business. Repressed grievances should be brought into the open now, which will result in a positive and real clearing of the air. And beware of a tendency to overindulge in good food or drink. During a SIX-transit you tend to take things too personally so it's easy to overdo, develop a lazy streak. Discipline is not one of your strong points now. Your talents are impressive and unique—don't overestimate them. What you feel and believe is worth more than what you earn and own.

Tips for Healthier Living During the SIX Year

The bones and spine are more vulnerable during the SIX Personal Year. And don't feel singled out if dietary plans need some perks and change as a tendency to put on weight is likely. Plenty of fresh air and sunshine in addition to outdoor physical activity could help offset the aforementioned.

Best times for elective surgery are the 4th and 8th months following your birthday. Obtain accurate medical advice on the 6th, 15th and the 24th of every month this year.

Serenity and good nature are definite assets toward having and maintaining good health this Year. However, along with the strengths come a few hazards—such as a tendency to overeat, under-exercise and allow your system to become sluggish as a result.

Don't pressure yourself—if you know your destination, you'll arrive when the time is right.

The ruby is the Personal Year SIX gemstone which symbolizes inner strength. The ruby influences success over controversies; the stone of love, valor and devotion. Your healing colors are lilac, blushing pink and lemon. Burn purple or yellow candles to enhance optimism.

Emotions, Love & Romance

Aim to understand the meaning of the word "relationship" this Year. You should find it easier to express affection even if you are normally tongue-tied. Communications between family members (including pets) is more successful. Get closer to stepchildren and in-laws.

Single parents find family matters mellowing throughout this transit although ex-spouses may not "pay up" until the approaching SEVEN or EIGHT cycle.

In-home young adults are likely to push your buttons, be more rebellious, move away. Communicate, don't coerce. You're more convincing, more clear, now.

On a whole, you should feel quite good and enjoy being with people. Make it clear to those around you that you are concerned for their welfare and that you are there to help. Chances are, they will feel the same about your welfare, too. Sympathy and support are SIX'S aspirins.

You won't want to be alone now, and may feel unable to operate without intimate support. Talk to others, per-

haps a therapist, about what's on your mind. Don't go it alone this Year. You won't succeed at everything—you must decide which areas of your life require special attention. Don't overtax your strength or your health.

Finances

During a SIX Year, you're inclined to spend money rather than build savings. It's excellent for financial-planning, obtaining accurate economic counseling. Get involved with an investment group, ask prosperous pals for tips, bounce ideas off buddies and welcome encouragement. Even if you're not involved in business, seek the advice of those whom you respect and are doing well.

Tax and legal problems are best handled throughout the 2nd and 10th months following your last birthday. Monies owed from children get repaid during SIX Years. But don't mistake pipe dreams for practical dollars.

The SIX favors real estate investment and redecorating, provided you're not too extravagant or self-indulgent. It's easy to fritter money away on impulsive purchases now—so watch it! Streamline ideals and goals.

Work is more fulfilling and enjoyable now, providing you a sense of purpose and structure. Quite often, this comes about through improved status, better conditions, or a new job with better pay. Making money is nothing to be ashamed of. In fact, it is a necessity. The SIX opens up your mind to new ways

of improving finances, so don't be afraid to put them into effect. Secure your future in the SIX.

How to Use the SIX Year to Your Fullest Advantage

You're not content to go it alone now. Get out and socialize, make new contacts. Your personality is more open and friendly and others respond warmly to you now.

Define issues with those you're intimately associated—lover, spouse or business partners. Together you will accomplish more than either could separately. You need other's input and assistance. Not because you're weak, but because they may enlighten you about your individuality now more than ever.

This is a Year of inner and outer equanimity. Take stock of yourself without getting caught up in the usual rush. Even if affairs are not going smoothly, the SIX delivers breathing space, more hope, fresh air. If you've been overworked or overstressed, you now have time to take it easy. If you are already relaxed and centered, you will feel even better. Be careful about passivity, sitting around waiting or for someone else to take the first step.

You are more romantic, affectionate. Smooth out difficulties that you've been having because they now see that you only want peace. People are willing to help you. There is plenty of time to correct problems, so go easy on yourself. Your instincts are working well; trust them.

THEMES FOR THE SEVEN PERSONAL YEAR

It's said that on the Seventh day God rested, so take a sabbatical from past upsets and hang ups. Your forecast-focus revolves around personal pursuits, paperwork, intellectual endeavors and travel. During this cycle, you'll find yourself analyzing everything and everyone and feel a strong need to be alone. This Year, you have plenty of energy to do the things you enjoy, but very little when it comes to routine chores. Rather than waste time, concentrate on doing what appeals to you.

Let everybody have their way as long as it doesn't interfere with you even if you don't agree with what they do or say. Don't buy into others' "stuff" or make compromises that go against your beliefs now. What transpires over the coming 12 months improves your bargaining power in both business and pleasure! Forget about ancient history; exorcise old demons, dispense with distractions and take control your future. While some things can be pushed to the limit, you don't deserve the drama.

However, the SEVEN Year can get you into trouble if you shift gears without thinking. You may overexpand, overextend, trust the wrong people or dumbly deviate from accepted paths. Heed all safety rules.

Old friends or business contacts suddenly pop back into your life now. Too many people may try to get involved in your day-to-day dreams, so you need to decide where to draw the line. Deal with them as honestly as possible. By giving too much of yourself away to others, you risk losing sight of a goal or ambition close to home.

Keywords & Phrases

- Self-discovery
- Get away from it all
- An emphasis on philosophy, law
- Education, credentials
- Inner growth
- The Seven Year-itch, travel

Shortcomings/Pitfalls

- Repression, resentment
- Brooding over the past
- Laziness, blaming others
- Scatter-brained, accident-prone
- Over-seriousness, self-indulgent
- Worrisome, melancholic

What to Expect

Something that has been worrying you for quite some time will have to be dealt with this Year, but once you get to the root of the problem, you'll no longer fear

the unknown. Don't put on a brave face. Let your feelings show. Clear away unnecessary clutter.

If your thinking is normally very rigid and inflexible, this may turn into a very upsetting period in which your beliefs are challenged and found wanting. Ideas and opportunities that you would never have entertained before become brighter. Travel, other cultures call your name.

You may suddenly discover that your friends of many years seem limited, narrow or no longer interesting. You will want to withdraw from the rapid pace of everyday existence in order to find peace, examine yourself, make alterations to your immediate surroundings. This number-transit stimulates the idealistic as well as the spiritual side of your personality. If you have any psychic inclinations, you will discover your intuitive abilities more aroused in the months ahead.

You now have greater compassion for the sufferings of others and want very much to do something about finding a solution to their hurts and pains. Don't be afraid to make whatever changes you feel are needed to put your (and their) world right. Refuse to let other's insecurities distort your priorities.

What to Avoid

This is a Year of major endings and beginnings, and you can't have one without the other. Don't get upset if someone important goes out of your life, because it will make room for someone who's going to be even more valuable to you in the Years to come.

The SEVEN is also a time of great activity where you live, because you are determined to have your surroundings exactly the way you want. Of course, if someone in the home has a different point of view about this, expect arguments as domestic strife is on the other side of this cyclic-coin. Living with parents or caring for elderly roommates may fan flames of dissention as well. If you cohabitate: cooperate, coordinate. Place and keep yourself in a position where you are free to change your mind because you'll do it frequently.

If you are in business for yourself, be careful not to grow too rapidly or overextend yourself. You will be tempted to risk-take because of your high spirits and optimism but you might leave yourself vulnerable. Beware of impulsiveness! Don't bluff your way out of problems, because you will end up in more of a mess than when you started. Don't blame yourself for other's shortcomings.

Tips for Healthier Living During the SEVEN Year

Treat your lungs better—experiment with deep-breathing exercises, get more fresh air. Stop smoking, walk, exercise. The SEVEN Year suggests setting time aside for meditation, relaxation and stress reducing—everyday. Because you're feeling more willing to experiment now, beware of weight gain.

Break free from old habits that damage or limit performance. Turn vital probabilities into possibili-

ties. Let your body grow and develop, now. Otherwise, be ready to pay The Piper this Year.

For the elderly, the SEVEN may signify the onset of a disorder that makes the conscious mind less acute or an illness that causes the mind to wander, withdraw from the world. Find and follow the recommendations of a competent physician throughout the coming 12 months.

SEVEN Year's healthful colors are pastels, particularly shades of green or blue. Burn light blue candles to enhance relaxation in your meditations. The gemstone Jade has strong links with self-discipline. In ancient times, it was believed to encourage moderation in drink and quell unruly passions. Jade is also reputed to have a calming influence and promote confidence when worn in a ring or pendant.

Your current health-style may not be ideal, but little by little, you are moving ahead.

Emotions, Love & Romance

Get ready to re-groove relationships—think seven-year itch. It's time to tie up loose ends, redefine your wants and needs. Although new romantic affairs may be transient, they will have a liberating effect and increase your capacity to experience life.

Someone will enter your life who will act as a "guru." He or she will open up many avenues that you have never before experienced or have neglected investing time. "Enlightenment" takes as many forms as there are teachers and students. Don't waste time worrying about events that may never occur. Tell yourself that anything is possible and you'll find that, almost by magic, it is!

New friendships or romances develop in the 2nd, 5th and 9th months after your last birthday.

Marriage or other close partnership will be challenged. During the SEVEN Year, you feel a need for secrecy. Even if you are concealing something for another's "own good," partners are not likely to see it that way and their confidence will be undermined.

Talks of divorce are likely to occur now. Be careful consulting others for advice, even professionals such as lawyers, marriage counselors or doctors. Whatever happens, do not suspend your own critical faculties just because someone else seems to be an "expert."

The SEVEN stimulates the idealistic side of your nature in beautiful ways, inviting you to see harmony and happiness in many things. But remain alert—you may fall madly in love with someone because they seem so perfect and ideal, although the truth may be quite different. You can chip away at a romantic problem for only so long before it must be tackled head-on. With no shortage of ideas on how to resolve the issue, you'll need to identify those with potential and those that are unrealistic.

Finances

Understand the rules of money-games and learn to play more skillfully, ethically. Don't live in Dollar-Doubt. The more you push, the more you'll profit.

SEVEN and EIGHT Years are "inheritance" and payback times. Those who owe, bestow. However, be on guard against gambling and lotteries as SEVEN Years do not bring speculative windfalls.

Illegal or below-board undertakings bring great problems. Analyze and fine-tune, grow slowly, reassess what you have. Conflicts with coworkers will arise if they feel threatened by your efforts to get ahead, so play down such encounters unless something real is at stake.

During the SEVEN Year, the more desperately you cling to what you think you own, the more likely you are to lose it. Loosen up and weigh all options. Look at your overall goals honestly and see what you have to do in order to achieve them. It's relatively easy to make necessary, realistic changes now. Plan and act wisely. Don't be pressured into going against your beliefs; recognize your true priorities.

Wednesday is your best day for job interviewing; send proposals, e-mail on Sunday evening.

How to Use Your Year to the Fullest

Bless your body, improve the mind, study and meditate—good advice for all, but especially for SEVEN Year folks. Discretion is an everyday necessity. Schedule frequent periods for seclusion. Whenever possible, travel, run away from routine. Seek out stimulating people, locales.

"Gut" feelings are more accurate now and you're able to intuit very subtle ideas and thoughts. This perception will prove helpful in your relationships with others. Avoid people who are negative because your increased sensitivity may make you an easy victim.

The SEVEN favors luck with and from lawyers, scholars, spiritual leaders and authors.

Favorable occurrences will not happen through "luck" in the usual sense this Year. Rather, it opens up and sharpens your mind in order that you see matters clearer, enabling you to turn it to your best advantage. There is nothing wrong with following your instincts; just be sure they are pointing you in the right direction.

Take time to recharge, exercise. The SEVEN applauds individualization and specialization. Correct past mistakes, strengthen friendships, get rid of waste. You can promise yourself the world, but unless you intend to keep your word and invest in yourself, all you'll wind up with is dirt.

THEMES FOR THE EIGHT PERSONAL YEAR

Hard work, personal magnetism, and discrimination deliver rewards in the EIGHT Year. Standing up to bullies, challenging competitors and showing others that you are fearless are your keys for success. Refuse to overestimate your abilities. Forget about ancient history: when you exorcise the demons of the past, you will control your future. There is more than one path. Show and tell others.

Don't let insecurities, sentiment or emotional doubt overwhelm you anymore. Organize, reorganize and be efficient in everything you do. Have faith in your abilities. Prosperity and cash-consciousness dominate EIGHT's stars when you allow hard work, follow-through and others assistance. Tradition and realism rules!

Let people and conditions work for you for a change. Be grand. Prove that you have commitment as well as vision. This Year, you develop more maturity and a deeper sense of who you are. Look to the 'tried and true' for inspiration. You will give much and demand equal in return now, whether in work or love. Refuse to buckle under! If you need to impress employers or other important people with your ideas and ambition, now is the time.

Employees of large institutions, government agencies and big industrial companies are favored during the EIGHT Year. Remember that a realistic view takes you farther than wishful thinking. Don't play games.

Keywords & Phrases
- Job advancements
- Taking care of business
- Inheritance or legacies
- Honor and awards
- Reaping what you've sown
- A fool and his money are soon parted

Shortcoming/Pitfalls
- Power-hungry; greedy
- Intolerance; arrogance
- Material obsession
- Jealousy
- Scheming
- "All talk, no action"

What to Expect
Financial decisions need to be made this Year and you shouldn't have too much trouble deciding what has to be done. The important thing is not to forget about your finances. Worrying will get you nowhere.

It's time for deliberate action, but beware of rushing into situations just because you can't wait to finish.

You're ambitious now, want to get on with life, make your mark, be the boss. It's pointless to let vague doubts or fears inhibit your progress. Transcend anxieties until they pass, then renew your efforts.

Your energy is more disciplined now. You are finally able to focus and work harder at various projects, whether physical or mental, and not give up until they're finished. Superiors and fellow employees will admire you for this, and you'll gain more credit than those who work in a grandiose but less thorough manner will.

This is the Year to make things secure, stable. If your expectations are overly optimistic, you may get disappointed, but the reasons will become clear quicker. You're now able to balance your emotional needs with your sense of obligation and duty. While you are aware of your feelings, don't let them overwhelm you. Your enthusiasm will take you through the next stage. It's unlikely that you will have to do any task over again, nor will anyone else have to clean up after you.

Dealings with the military or the government and those who work with steel, iron or tools go well. Building structures, doing household repairs get the thumbs up. Job interviewing goes best on Thursdays.

What to Avoid

Keeping up with the Jones' and spending money like there's no tomorrow is common in an EIGHT Year. Don't be a tightwad or paranoid about money or status. Any anxieties you feel about your future owe more to personal insecurities than to any genuine concerns.

Your tastes now lean towards the elegant, and you may be tempted to buy items that are out of your budget. Watch tendencies to waste or squander. Stay on top, keep things under control. Working with others may be frustrating, because it is hard for you to maintain a slow pace.

Beware of bullying cohorts this Year. Unfortunately, aggressiveness and abrasive actions occur. More often than not, you may put people off by acting in a dictatorial manner. Demonstrate patience this Year; don't antagonize.

This number-transit signifies an inflated ego, a state of mind in which you may spend money beyond your means. Don't take on more than you can handle. Balance your daring with reason and care. Your current lifestyle may not be ideal, but little by little, you are moving forward!

**Tips for Healthier Living
During the EIGHT Year**

Too much stress is harmful, so don't feel guilty about delegating certain responsibilities and, when necessary, discarding some. The digestive track, constipation, hemorrhoids and fertility are Number EIGHT issues. Concerns about bones, knees, or teeth may also take the spotlight.

The two gemstones synonymous with the EIGHT

Year: the garnet, associated with victory in competitive endeavors and topaz, reportedly for attracting wealth and pleasant dreams plus generosity from patrons. Wear or display them proudly.

You're now in a position to make long-overdue shifts in your eating and lifestyle. Stop compromising what you know is right. It's easy to get trapped on a treadmill—the time is ripe to prove you can get off.

Best months for medical exams, elective or corrective surgeries and getting accurate second-opinions are during the 1st, 5th, 7th, and 10th after your birthday.

Emotions, Love & Romance

It is one thing to know what or whom you want and quite another to have the courage to pursue it. During an EIGHT Year, mentors, folks older than yourself as well as those with influence, power and wealth enter your life. Your desires, like fine wine, become more refined.

You're in a splendid position for an ongoing romance or to develop a new one. Don't let your inherent caution prevent you from chasing moonbeams. But be careful not to jump to conclusions, be too hasty or react negatively by demands made by others. It would be a shame to let confused thinking distract you from your personal happiness. Refuse to make blanket decisions based on how you felt in the past. Double-check doubts!

You are now able to put up with considerable adversity and strain because the EIGHT Year imbues strength and patience. However, there will times when you feel the need to be off by yourself to collect your thoughts rather than discuss them openly with partners. If you have a problem, seek out one whom you respect and can provide proper emotional support, practical solutions.

You're more in touch with your feelings and moods now. The starkness of emotions the EIGHT Year delivers may make you feel isolated. It's a contemplative time, when quiet brings comfort. Recharge when retreating. Don't deny yourself this satisfaction. Since Eight ushers in a period of nostalgia, welcome reunions with past lovers or old school friends.

Finances

EIGHT governs material resources and possessions. Issues regarding credit ratings, loans, prestige or honors take the spotlight. This is an excellent Year for hiring a financial planner, getting to know your accountant better and taking necessary steps to be a top money manager. It is far more important to ensure that finances are secure and that any temporary hiccup is just that: temporary.

Don't take on too much for the sake of impressing those in power. Success is never guaranteed, but you're now within reach of a long-term objective. Keep your wits and avoid messing up things. Be fair, and make sure that your interests are well protected.

EIGHT favors joining organizations and societies

that introduce you to influential persons. Promotions, favors and opportunity are to be expected. Don't pay top dollar for what you desire: shop around—even though this is a time for inheritance and lottery winnings.

The EIGHT is the number of "karma"—what you sow, you get. What you give freely to others will return sooner than later. Handle your duties and leave time to enjoy yourself.

How to Use Your EIGHT Year to the Fullest

The EIGHT Personal Year puts you in good standing with peers. With care, planning and restraint, it's a time of fortunate action, taking advantage of the moment. With finances moving to center stage, take serious steps towards self-improvement.

Stay calm—impulsive actions create havoc now. Remain cool and collected in everything you do. This is a time of triumph over obstacles, accomplishing goals. "Keep your head."

If you are in business for yourself, be careful not to expand too rapidly or overextend yourself because you're exposed to others in power. Protect your losses by not trying to impress those whom you cannot afford. Re-examine your goals. Make the most of eagerness—and stay centered!

What transpires this Year will alter your view of who you are. It will also urge you to uncover new ways to reach your financial goals. Opening doors is not enough—make sure they're the right ones.

The influence of the tarot card The Magician (see chapter four) is in effect throughout the One Personal Year. Here are the tarot cards for the remaining years: The High Priestess during Year Two, The Empress throughout Year Three, The Emperor over the months of Year Four, The Hierophant in Year Five, The Lovers in Year Six, The Chariot during Year Seven, Justice in Year Eight, and The Hermit throughout Personal Year Nine. Meditate on each throughout your Personal Year birthday cycle.

THEMES FOR THE NINE PERSONAL YEAR

It's house-cleaning time now—inner and outer! The NINE Year urges you to get rid of unnecessary habits, jobs and people. "Bye-bye" time. Instincts and intellect begets rewards. View situations from an "I will survive" perspective. You may have to compromise for the sake of progress or peace. Far from being defeatist, it's your smartest option. Make amends and move on.

Be prepared for emergencies because more-than-your-average amount of obstacles are likely to crop up and appear to block your ascent. Declare your intentions to everyone and cast away time-robbing activities, futile experiments, or pastimes that are taking you nowhere. You've paid your dues and done your time—now go out and blow your own horn!

Make an inventory of what you want and no longer need, and focus on what you need to be happy. Bring things to culmination. Sadly, this is a Year of loss—whether a job, death of a loved one, bankruptcy.

The NINE-transit favors solving mysteries, meditation, spiritual matters and learning. If ever there's a time to change your tactics and put to flight those who are taking your kindness for granted, this is it!

Keywords & Phrases
- "Out with the old"
- Endings
- Dreams fulfilled
- Fine-tune; reconcile
- Seek solace
- Make every moment count

Shortcomings/Pitfalls
- Sentimentality
- Whining, escapism
- Self-destructive
- Over-commitment
- Revenge
- Isolation; rebelliousness

What to Expect
This frantic phrase prompts sacrifice and eliminating the trivial. That you don't seem to be quite on the same wavelength as partners and loved ones is painfully obvious now. Innovation replaces habit. Play the game rather than worry about the odds; concentrate on the end rather than the means.

Your ability to cut through superficial details and get to the root of your difficulties will prove invaluable. Base decisions on facts rather than

dreams. The NINE Year delivers a powerful and positive maturing influence; in other words, you become wiser. As you are exposed to a broader world, your views about life will change.

Don't dominate anyone, even if you feel that it's for his or her own good. Existing relationships are intensified now because your needs are heightened and you require answers, gratification. You're changing . . . slowly yet profoundly. Throughout the NINE Year, you may feel that you are working very hard and that nothing is coming of it. Persevere. Put your points across clearly and don't let anyone interfere with your long-term security and happiness.

Don't take yourself so seriously that every challenge of position seems to be a threat. Remain calm. See what is really happening and cultivate broader outlooks. Don't hold on to people or things. Life is not a problem to be solved, but a reality to be experienced.

What to Avoid

Crying, kicking and screaming, or wallowing in self-pity in order to get your way won't cut the cake. Follow your heart, but use your head as well.

The time is right for dealing with serious matters; avoid the frivolous or meaningless. The Big Picture and bottom lines are what matters now. Keep an open mind, don't force your point of view on others (as you'll be inclined). Look within. With the NINE's influences enabling you to see things as they really are, you're better able to plan for the future instead of living in the past.

Because deception from others is on the rise, make sure that everything you do is strictly legitimate. Don't act ruthlessly or underhandedly toward others, even though you may feel they deserve to be beaten or are wrong. Enemies make themselves seen and heard. Don't get sidetracked by emotions or how things were in the old days.

Don't waste time or money this Year. Neither a borrower nor a lender be. Be careful of too many irons in the fire and don't get talked into doing anything you don't believe in. Speak your mind—the result will be sighs of relief.

Tips for Healthier Living During the NINE Year

You need to feel 100 percent right now—which means cutting down on stress, monitoring fitness or change of diet.

It's easier to over-do during the NINE transit. Brainstorm with your physician and insure that you are properly nourished. Because your imagination is on overdrive, fears may be groundless. Make a concerted attempt to work on your anxieties. Realism wins over wishful thinking.

Accidents are on the increase now. Pay attention to explosives, guns, sharp objects or cutting tools, especially. Watch your driving!

You may feel more tired, as if the burdens of life are too much. Traditionally, the NINE makes one feel old or world-weary, even if they are in fact young. While

some things can be pushed to the limit, remember that you cannot. The NINE Year of ten aggravates heart disease, colitis, ulcers and other tension disorders.

Grape and violet are your health giving colors this Year. Burn light blue candles to attract good health and mental alertness. Vanilla bath salts enhance meditation.

Your lucky gemstone is aquamarine. Ancient Romans believed this gem enhances happiness and soothes stomach, bowel or liver ailments. It is associated with compassion and wisdom. Display one on your desk or altar.

Emotions, Romance & Love

Why force passion when a subtle approach could be more effective? It's time for reflection, letting things take their natural course now. No one person's word is gospel—including yours. Accept the fact that some colleagues are out for themselves and for all they can get. Keep up your guard! What you discover in quiet contemplation will far outweigh what you have to give up socially.

Spend quality time alone and explore how you really feel about intimate matters. Your emotions and imaginations are intense and may influence your perception so much that it is hard to escape them. Broaden your horizons and don't repeat patterns that tossed you into disadvantage.

Loneliness is a big issue at this time. You may feel that any sort of union exists at the cost of your freedom or individuality. The need to be yourself is on the rise! Don't be afraid to let go, eliminate, or consolidate. Concentrate on what you do best. Don't say too much when you are at a loss for words.

A non-possessive live-and-let-live attitude is best during the NINE Year. Don't preach or take anything for granted. Pay attention and be conscious of what is happening. Everything is changing now—but this is not a time to reopen old wounds, repeat prior patterns.

Finances

The NINE Year is about renovating y-o-u in order to move forward. Don't be driven by outsiders. Take the initiative but don't overcommit. Even if you normally do not take risks, this transit may cause unexpected expenses or financial shortages because your feet aren't on the ground. More is at stake than material gains; you must be in the right frame of mind if you are to reap your just rewards.

This is a favorable time for dealing with authorities because they are more open to your ideas now. Legal interests are favored—more so regarding finding hidden loopholes, options. Sever outdated connections and safeguard your own financial interests! There is more going on than meets the eye. Delegate and discard.

You've been cramming so much into your life over the past two years that you're in danger of losing sight of your personal goals. However finely tuned your sense of responsibility may be, your only duty right now is to yourself. Job interviewing, investments prosper during the 4th and 8th months after your recent birthday. If handled properly, it will enhance your income.

Don't let an old responsibility dominate your life or allow pride to get in the way of destiny.

How to Use Your Personal NINE Year to the Fullest

A long-term ambition is about to enter a new phrase. When the opportunity arises, don't be afraid to make changes to your life. Remaining too long in one place will cause almost anyone to stagnate. Don't underestimate your abilities. The NINE Year delivers new experiences as a result from culling the old.

Save mundane tasks for another time—think "future." Be careful about overextending yourself or living beyond your resources. No one expects you to achieve the impossible (but you'll probably try anyway). Unload, clear out. It's a splendid time to turn good ideas into profitable enterprises: do so!

It's a Year for obtaining insight and understanding from elders. Finally, your emotions are more mature and you have a clearer perspective.

You're now inclined to question what others tell you. Don't believe everything you are told or take things for granted. You're not content to follow the same goals. Look more compassionately at yourself, the world and other people. Decide before you discard. Avoid taking too much on trust.

CHAPTER THREE

PALM READING: YOUR FUTURE IS IN YOUR HANDS

> **I was taught very early that I would have to depend entirely upon myself; that my future lay in my own hands.**
>
> —Darius Ogden Mills

After I've examined the sample of handwriting and did my magical math for upcoming Personal Years, I take a peek at the palms. All are unique. Is your partner caring, affectionate—perhaps you admire his or her long, slender palm and fingers? Is your client's spouse a louse—crude or predictable? Look to squarish-stinted-in-length digits. Are the palms filled with loads of lines? If so: you've got an emotional firecracker at your fingertips!

Add to all the insights of the previous chapters and note what follows. Everybody's hands are different. However, we all want the same things: happiness, health, love. Some obtain their "earnings" differently. What about you? Your client? Your family?

Unlike mathematics, where two and two always equal four, palmistry is not an exact science. It is an ancient global folk tradition suggesting character, emotional nature and personality from the shape and markings on the hand.

Greek thinkers such as Aristotle, Plato and Ptolemy saw great significance in the hand and regarded them as a valuable tool for understanding character. Virgil and Antonin the Pious and Julius Caesar and Augustus were skilled hand analysts. Josephus, the Jewish historian, wrote that Caesar was so accomplished that it was "impossible for any whose palm he had seen to deceive him in any way; in fact, one day, an individual came to him claiming to be Alexander son of Herod, and Caesar promptly recognized him as an imposter with no mark of royalty on his hand."

Although twenty-first century palmistry doesn't acknowledge a particular marking as signaling one who sits in a throne and rules a nation, there is more to this handicraft than meets the eye.

Each hand differs in numerous ways but there are, to pardon the pun, specific rules of thumb for delineating traits. As an astrologer and metaphysical researcher of 25 years, I have updated much of the old-fashioned jargon and fated forecasts.

RIGHT-LEFT HAND DIFFERENCE

Over 85 per cent of the world's population eat, write, and work with their right hands. Less than 100 years ago, left-handers were considered "sinister," and backward. In many cultures today around the world, to not have right hand dominance means ignorance. Until recently, most left-handers were forced to write with their right hands in American schools. Newspapers plastered headlines in 1993 about the high suicide rates of left-handed persons versus right.

To a modern palm-analyst, people with right hand dominance are stronger in their development of reasoning powers, logic, practicality and logical thinking. Left-handed individuals favor intuition, hunches and are more original in their thinking. Like Albert Einstein, many lefties are ambidextrous—skilled with both hands—having to adapt to a "right-handed world." It's interesting to note that stutterers are more frequently left-handed, as are slow learners.

Nevertheless, you generally use one hand more than the other.

Which is *your* dominant hand?

Regardless which one you use more regularly, concentrate on the markings and signs of your right hand with this book. To the modern palmist, the left-hand reveals your personal, private side—fantasies, hopes, dreams and when alone in the bathroom after a shower—warts and all.

The right hand tells how you present yourself to the outside world of daily life.

Let's next explain the hand's geography.

The **palm** consists of the area with lines and fleshy elevations below the fingers and is called the **front of the hand**. The **back of the hand** is where the knuckles and fingernails appear.

People with **small hands** see the overall, general picture but often overlook important details. Small hands think big! You are single-minded and pursue each goal with dogged determination and power, using reason and intellect rather than intuition. It's difficult to steer you off-course once you've made up your mind. You have the self-discipline to put aside immediate gratification for long-range achievement. You want accomplishment and a steady climb to security and status most of all, and may sacrifice home life and intimacy for long-term aims.

Big hands reveal sensitivity, versatility, and curiosity. While small hands skim the newspaper headlines, large hands enjoy the small print and cartoons. Full of mental energy, you are aggressive about getting what you want but flexible enough to see another point of view, instinctively knowing how to reach people on their own terms. You enjoy examining and categorizing others, always asking a million questions. What upsets you the most is not knowing the answer, dealing with stupidity from someone else and being told that there is only one way for you to do something.

Medium hands are good mediators between small-handed and big-handed people. Nimble-witted, and responsive, you shrug off daily upsets without too

much hassle and are not easily rocked off center. You pride yourself on not showing prejudice, you're practical—rejecting what is unsuitable, unhealthy or unnecessary. You enjoy things that make you feel warm and cozy. You go for serenity, comfort and the good things of life.

Is your **palm thin, slim?** The hand with **a thin palm** is the thinking and feeling hand. **Thin hands** are those of thoughts and concepts. You enjoy brainstorming, talking, and have an agile mind. You're bright, quick, and curious and very changeable in your moods. Full of mental and emotional energy, you want to know everything about everybody. You value rationality above all else, so when confronted with an emotional crisis, you try to reason things out and make the most logical choice. Instinct and gut reactions get pushed aside in favor of logical constructs, although your instinctive response is often right on target.

Is your palm **"square-ish,"** like a child's building block? The hand with **the square palm** is the practical hand**.** You take nothing for granted and demand that facts be laid on the table. You possess good reasoning abilities and have a need for security. You're a person that shrugs off day-to-day upsets and are not easily rocked off center. You're a person of action, a hard-worker, a doer, and achiever. Law-and-and-order and no-nonsense is your code of honor. You say what you think but may have difficulty seeing another point of view. You can be extremely critical but

demand no more from others than you expect from yourself. You need to be needed and get emotional satisfaction from being productive and useful.

Most palms are a melange of square and thin but on closer examination, one type usually outweighs the other, and provides the key to your character.

The degree of **flexibility** of the fingers tells how adaptable you are. Ideally, the fingers should arch gently backward under pressure. If they don't bend back at all, it's difficult for you to give in and see the other person's side of the story. Real stiff means real stingy—arthritis city. When they flex back real easily, arching way back, you'll do anything to avoid an argument. What the French call *souplesse* is beauty in motion.

No specific metric measurement explains what constitutes **short and long fingers.** Their length must be judged in relation to the length of the palm itself. Relativity is what Mr. Einstein discovered all around us.

Do your **fingers appear short** in relation to the palm? Short fingered-folk decide matters quickly, act fast and understand the larger scheme of things. Unfortunately, **short fingered-people** don't always take time to think matters through, acting abruptly and, at times, reckless. You are not given to emotional display, and tend to overlook details—judging the big picture, rather than minutiae. Thinking is unplanned and actions are erratic. You're impatient, always in a rush. Prone to be childish and stubborn, things you don't understand make you angry.

Very short fingers tend towards carelessness. Active and vital, you're easily bored by routine and need to be constantly busy. Emotions tend to get in the way of action, so therefore, you can become a bit childish about getting your needs met—*your* way! Enjoying control, taking a back seat to others' whims makes you nervous.

Long fingers take their time doing things and fuss over details and the "why" and "how come?" in matters. Planning, analyzing, discussing, and asking questions are important for you. You enjoy examining and categorizing situations. You don't fear

compromise or demonstrating affection and emotions. Security means understanding something and having it so scoped-out you can explain it to anyone else. You have an instinct for putting yourself into others' shoes.

Thick, fleshy fingers reveal a sensual, erotic, passive nature. You enjoy good food, luxury and may be a bit of a couch potato. Beulah, peel me a grape! **Thin fingers** mean that you think matters out before acting and that you're inclined to be a bit nervous.

Fingers with **prominent knuckles** (not caused by arthritis) signify reasoning abilities whether the fin-

gers are long or short. You are a problem-solver who uses logic, taking time to carefully weigh pros and cons. Large knuckles suggest objectivity, patience, and good rationale.

Smooth fingers with an absence of knuckles belong to people who use intuition more than reason, You play your hunch rather than status quo logic.

Fingertips come in specific shapes and are judged from the palm rather than the manicured nail-side of the hand. Some hands carry more than one shape. Always note which shape is dominant.

Pointed fingers reveal curiosity and a good imagination. A dreamy, sensitive escapist, you possess a rich fantasy life and enjoy being in love and nurturing others. Although not technically artistic, you appreciate the arts, music, and the finer things of life. It's essential to have someone who loves and needs you, whether a mate, child, a plant or Pekinese.

Rounded fingertips enjoy people, are receptive and react to outside stimuli. Rarely do round fingertip-types like living alone. The constant presence of someone who cares for you makes your world safe and desirable.

Blunt, squarish fingertips are not spontaneous folks. "What's in it for me?" is apt to be your song. You gain emotional satisfaction from being careful, orderly, useful, and productive. You crave stability above all else, often viewing change as undesirable or threatening. You enjoy clearly defined gender roles, job descriptions, deadlines.

Fingertips that resemble a cook's spatula or Japanese fan—flared at the tip, tapering towards the knuckle—love physical activity and, usually, the great outdoors.

Spatulate fingertips enjoy a challenge and are excited by new conquests. You are vivacious, lively, and a bit restless. You gain great satisfaction from doing and making things and are easily bored. Waiting around for slow pokes or listening to long debates is not your cup of tea. Not a lover of detail, you're better with facts rather than philosophy.

A long palm with long fingers enjoys talking things out but may get hung up on small details and miss the big picture. Intuitive and sensitive to others, it's easy to put yourself into another's shoes, often putting others first and ignoring your own best interests. Not an aggressive or overly physical person, you work well in creative arenas.

People with **long palms and short fingers** tend to be argumentative and have made-up minds before the facts are on the table. You are impatient with your emotions and those of others because, to you, feelings get in the way of things you want to do. Anger and irritability come easy but you don't stay mad for long because you want to get on to the next thing. A bit of an extrovert, you're well suited for careers that involve change, assertiveness and adventure.

A short palm with short fingers are down to earth, logical souls who work well in the daily grind of the material world. Preferring a stable and predictable

life-style, you dislike change, are self-sufficient and aggressive about getting what you need. Punctual and straightforward, you see things in an uncomplicated manner and are well suited for careers in agriculture or horticulture, mechanical jobs and those where you focus on one thing at a time.

The short palm with long fingers are mentally alert, insatiably curious, and enjoy exchanging opinions and ideas. Like a detective, putting together a puzzle's pieces stimulates you. You emphasize thinking, language, research, and take time to explain things. You are intelligent, have no fear of intellectual challenge and enjoy people who are voluble verbally. Well-mannered and diplomatic in speech, you rarely lose your temper and always try to avoid arguments. You weigh the strengths and weaknesses in matters and make judgements based on facts without letting feelings get in the way. You would do well in fields of communication, teaching, publishing, or public relations.

ABOUT FINGERNAILS

The fingertips have more nerve endings than in any other of the body. This multitude of small nerve endings is shielded by your fingernail armor. With age and poor health, their texture becomes **thin, brittle or broken**. Fingernails come in all shapes and sizes but their shape remains fixed from birth and provides clues to personality. The study of fingernail shapes and their traits is known as onyxology.

A healthy nail looks smooth as glass, is pliable and elastic with a visible semicircle —called a "moon"— at the nail bed. Moons wax and wane, growing in size when you exercise and when vitality is good, shrinking below the nail-bed when your recuperative powers may be weak. A healthy nail is straight or convex, not sunken or pockmarked. The skin beneath should have a rosy pink glow.

Nails that are **small** in proportion to their fingers suggest a person who burns the candle at both ends and runs on nervous energy. You are impulsive, curious but quick to lose your temper. Your mind is active and fast but you have difficulty sticking with anything for long. In your headlong rush to uncover facts, you sometimes overlook important bits of data or are careless in your research.

Small and squarish nails dominate conversations. It is important for you to be recognized and express yourself in some dramatic way. Your thoughts are usually focused on yourself and you can be extremely self-centered. Although rather charming, it's hard for you to see the other another's point of view because your opinion alone counts. Your style is forceful and energetic.

Large nails that take up lots of the top-third of a finger are big thinkers. You believe in hard work and enjoy challenge. Once you decide you want something, you are not easily distracted or discouraged and often succeed because of persistence and single-mindedness. You project an image of confidence, vitality, self-efficiency and yearn to be to recognized (and

admired) by one and all. You are strongly sexual and sensual, but only fulfilled within the structure of a committed relationship.

Thin, skinny nails are critical people who are extremely tough on themselves and everybody else. You have a strong sense of self, but little understanding of those around you. You plan carefully actions and aren't likely to do anything on impulse. You are reluctant to behave forcefully, keeping your anger in check. This defensiveness and critical manner often stems from feeling inadequate and a fear of intimacy. Afraid of being rejected, you might shut yourself off from others or refuse to get involved because you fear getting hurt.

Oval egg-shaped nails are the most common shape. You are social-minded and take things as they come. Your passions never rule your thinking and you rarely act in haste or anger. You are very aware of what other people think and are inclined to conform to majority rules. You often have difficulty asserting yourself and going after what you want in a direct or decisive manner. You don't deal well with confrontations, or physical combat. You like to make friends, not adversaries.

Almond-shaped nails are dreamers, lovers and sometime martyrs. You enjoy color, music, beauty and art in all forms, and want to fill your life with lovely things. Not money-minded like an accountant, you ask about prices because you hate to deny yourself anything, often running into debt. Highly sensitive,

you cannot bear to see anyone hurt (especially yourself) and you identify with struggling artists, the weak and deprived, underdogs.

Long, rounded nails reveal a tolerant, understanding person who often neglects their own needs, putting loved ones first. You prefer to do things with others and enjoy a peaceful home filled with music art and laughter. You're the dabbling sort who likes to try anything once. Mentally agile, you learn quickly and enjoy sharing what you learn. **Long nails with squared-off bottoms** are less experimental and prefer facts, stability, predictability. Expressing emotions is difficult for you and it's hard for you to relax, unwind, and let your hair down. You show concern for others by doing practical, necessary things.

Wide nailed folks make discriminating, practical choices but tend to get argumentative and set in their ways. It's difficult for you to see another point of view. You dislike criticism and prefer to do things your way. Security and stability are very important to you. A lover of routine and schedule, once you find the perfect job or partner, you tend to stay for life.

Square-appearing nails need lives that run with logic, schedule, and clockwork precision and are lovers of routine, order, and common sense. You build carefully for the future and make certain that everything you do is build on a solid foundation and on precedent facts. You perform your duties efficiently and modestly and derive a sense of satisfaction helping someone else.

Nails with visible ridges or indented "ripples" flag the worrywart. Emotions are confusing and high anxiety. Almost too compassionate and needing love, you have great difficulty drawing the line with dependent people. A dreamer, you often get so mired in your fantasies that you forget the mundane world of paying bills, doing homework. You demean your abilities and are highly critical of yourself.

Horizontal ridges across the nail, called "gutters," suggest weak recuperative powers and melancholy. Easily hurt, you fear nothing you do will make things better and often give up without trying. Talk things out with others, reach out.

FINGERPRINTS

Dermatoglyphics is what doctors and palmists call the study of skin engravings. Like Egyptian hieroglyphics, these fine ridges and patterns that cover the palms and fingertips as well as the soles of your feet are also read and interpreted. Like zebras and snowflakes, no two hands, finger or footprints are exactly alike, often differing between the right and left of the same individual as well as sets of identical twins.

Fingerprint identification was first used by Sir Francis Galton in police work in the 1800s. In addition to identifying an individual, they are also associated with particular behavior traits.

Fingerprints form five months before you are born and grow as you grow in age and size, but never change their original pattern. There are three basic types that account for approximately 80 percent of all fingerprint patterns, each marked with dozens of details and variations. Fingerprints represent the most basic and unchangeable elements of your personality and never change. Palmists place great importance on the thumb print and note which design is predominant on both hands.

The **loop fingerprint** resembles a cowboy's lasso. A majority of loops reveal that you are adaptable, agreeable, and don't like to rock the social boat. You make the most of every situation and are very aware of the status quo. Because you're concerned about what other's think, you have difficulty expressing your true feelings and opinion. Communication in all its myriad forms appeals to you and you maintain a large circle of associates and acquaintances. You speak with them frequently and stay in touch with those who live far away via letter, telephone, or fax. Mentally agile and clever, you learn quickly.

The **whorl** looks like the bulls-eye of an archery target and is the sign of the individualist. Self-expression is important and you especially enjoy exploring new ideas and concepts. You don't believe just because everyone else does. Conventional wisdom and accepted truths don't hold much water and you are eager to contest them with original ideas of your own. Even though your ideas and dreams may be grandiose or unrealistic, you believe they are possible. Impossible dreams last a lifetime. Somewhat of a flatterer, you are charming and enjoy the concept of romance and being in love.

SMALL

SMALL SQUARISH

LARGE

THIN SKINNY

OVAL

ALMOND

LONG ROUNDED

LONG

WIDE

SQUARE

RIDGES

HORIZONTAL RIDGES

LOOP

WHORL

ARCH

In July 1994, Professor Peter Pharoah of the UK Medical Research Center in England proclaimed that the shape of a fingerprint is the sign of a healthy heart and can predict whether the disease is in your future. Professor Pharoah says that you may be prone to high blood pressure, a major cause of heart disease, when you have an abnormal high number of those tight circular ridges called whorls. The more fingers with whorls, the higher the risk and the closer you should watch your cholesterol and fat intake.

Looking like an upside-down capital letter "T," the **Arch** is commonly found on the fingers of efficient, hard-working and reliable people. Your mind works in an orderly and organized fashion. It's hard for you to take anything at face value—you quickly begin dissecting it to see what makes it tick. You have a good memory for facts, figures and words and could use your keen analytical ability in such fields as auto repair, accounting, book editing, computer programming, or research. Cautious and conservative in your ideas and opinions, you are a follower rather than an intellectual pioneer, comfortable with the tried-and-true.

The composite fingerprint is the term used when two or more patterns "blend" into one another. In this case, note the dominant image.

WRIST LINES

Lines that circle the wrist are called rasclettes or wristlets. Three clear, distinct lines denote great physical strength and endurance. Money and possessions give you a sense of security and you enjoy great pleasure seeing a job well done. You plan carefully and work hard. **Rasclettes pointed upwards into the palm** denote vanity and a love of mirrors. This is also shows a love of children and animals. You spend more time dreaming rather than doing when you have **three broken rasclettes**. Your wonderful imagination enables you to "see" things others don't. In a woman, however, this is may signal possible problems with pregnancy.

FINGERS

Each finger is named after an ancient mythological deity or heavenly planet, and tells a different story.

The **index finger** is named Jupiter and reveals your leadership abilities and how assertive you are. The **middle** finger is Saturn and denotes how you learn things and how disciplined you are. Venus, the **ring finger** reveals your style, flair and personal happiness with work and appreciation of the arts. The **little finger** is called Mercury and deals with how you communicate and learn, your wits. The **thumb** bespeaks of individuality, perseverance, and sense of self-worth and is called Uranus.

The **index finger is considered to be long** when it rises above the nail base of the middle finger. This suggests star quality, belief in yourself. You test your own limits and believe that you never know what you can do until you try. You take pride in yourself and

your accomplishments. You are tough to ignore when you have something to say. You have a strong sense of self and always seek new ways to do things.

When the **index and middle fingers are nearly the same length**, you enjoy being the boss and in control. You possess a strong sense of the dramatic and can be quite flamboyant in the way you go about expressing yourself. You magnify your emotions in order to get attention and act larger than life.

When your **index finger is shorter than the ring finger**, you prefer to follow rather than lead. You need to be needed and gain emotional satisfaction from being helpful. You don't enjoy being the center of attention or having too many responsibilities. Easily hurt, this extraordinarily sensitivity may make you take a backseat to others. Conservative, traditional and spiritual in your beliefs, you are inclined to follow established philosophies and faiths. You can't stand to see anything or anyone suffer. This keen sensitivity enables you to feel a kinship with all living things, plants, and animals alike.

A long, straight and proud-standing middle finger reveals a love for schedule. You're serious about your commitments and don't mind being alone. Work is very important to you and you're happiest when situations are orderly and structured. You possess natural managerial abilities and are known for shrewdness, diligence, and reliability. Although you are ambitious, status and recognition is not as important as honor and personal happiness.

Middle fingers are considered short when they only reach the top of the ring finger. Stick to what you know rather than taking chances on new ideas or practices. You are rather old-fashioned, conservative. You hold on to your resources and want to make it on your own rather than rely on others. Taking risks is difficult for you.

Bent or curved middle fingers are the sign of the collector and one who hoards and save things. Your physical home and personal belongings represent security and stability to you. Highly critical of yourself, you might lack a sense of self-worth or undervalue your abilities.

A middle finger with pronounced knuckles says that learning and pushing yourself to be a good scholar is one of your greatest assets. You have plenty of common sense about finances but have trouble with mundane things like remembering where you left your keys. You are defensive about your rights and fear loss of individual choice, apprehensive that your independence will be hampered by authority figures or too many laws.

When the **tip of the middle finger is spatulate**, like an inverted triangle or paddle, a love of the outdoors, gardening, and science is noticed. You have an inextricable bond with nature, your friends and animals and are a staunch defender of equal rights and fair play. You have no desire to behave aggressively or engage in combat with others, tend to be withdrawn and have a problem asserting yourself.

Venus, **the ring finger**, is concerned with personal joy, happiness and an appreciation of music and the arts. A **straight ring finger reaching above the nailbed of the middle finger** says that you don't fear showing your feelings. Caring for someone makes your world safe and desirable. When your ring finger is **longer than the index finger**, you crave applause and approval and enjoy the niceties money can buy. You may not be especially facile with words but you communicate well with color, fashion, and visual stimuli. You like crowds, sharing your thoughts and being in the limelight.

Watch your disbursements and your bank check's balance if the **ring finger is m-u-c-h longer than the middle**. Gambling instincts prevail! You don't "see" risks clearly in speculation. Your eyes are bigger than your stomach in money management. Despite great charisma and grand visions, your economic savvy is unrealistic. Conversations with you often revolve around your latest accomplishments and acquisitions.

Three or more lines running vertically below the ring finger are called **Venus Lines**. You have the rare ability to see both sides of a situation and have more than one career interest. Always tactful and diplo-

matic in speech, you're open for new avenues to make money and prosper. You'll always have money when you need it, thanks usually to the good graces and goodwill of others. **More than four vertical lines below** the ring finger, say you have a tendency to be a jack-of-all trades, master of none. Mentally hyperactive, you're full of ideas but short on focus and may have trouble bringing your ideas down to earth or applying them in practical ways.

A long little finger, called Mercury, reaching above the ring finger's top knuckle, reveals that you think big and talk well. Optimistic and adventuresome, your enthusiasm is contagious. By and large, you're an optimist and you learn quickly and demonstrate an eagerness to get things done. **Long Mercury fingers** make fine speakers, singers, and musicians. **A square-tipped little finger** says that you speak (and, argue) well, and state your case with clear intent. You could be a good judge, umpire, lawyer because you act from equality and fairness.

The spade-tipped little finger endears audiences with warmth and charisma. You are conservative, don't like causing friction and are inclined to do what is "expected." At best, you're open-minded; at worst, vacillating and overly accommodating. Friendship and approval is more important to you than romance or saying what you feel.

Vertical lines on the fleshy area below the little finger suggest you are good at decision-making, see things logically and would make a good doctor or nurse. You pride yourself on your efficiency and dedication to duty and can usually be depended on to get the job done. **A little finger that "bends" away from the hand** suggests an inability to get along with people but a good ear for language, music, and rhythm. Your focus on individual details often causes you to miss the larger picture.

The thumb reveals how you express yourself, your individuality and your willingness to change and it's named for Uranus. **A long thumb** reaches up to the middle joint of the index finger. This is the sign a strong ego and healthy sense of who you are: always ready with a word of encouragement, genuinely joyous in making people happy. You feel secure in a commanding position. You seem to never grow tired and often burn the candle at both ends. Pride keeps you from becoming overly dependent on others.

A very short thumb that doesn't reach the bottom of the index finger says you are also short on willpower and follow-through. You have problems making up your mind. It's difficult for you to separate yourself from other's needs and desires. Too compassionate, you don't know how or when to draw the line with people who drag you. You're easy to get along with but must learn to say "no," "nada," "nein," and "never again" in several foreign languages. A Berlitz blitz.

You're able to see another's point of view and give freely when the **tip of your thumb bends back easily**. If the thumb arches freely backward, you do what

others tell you and are overly concerned about the thoughts of the neighbors. Your heart rules your head and may have trouble making rational decisions. Very sentimental and a bit unrealistic, it's difficult for you to "live and let live." **An inflexible, stiff-tipped thumb** makes you argumentative, overly set in your ways. You pride yourself on getting the job done... *your* way. A pragmatist, you rarely take chances with time or money. Your friendships may be few, but they are usually forever.

Does the angle of your **thumb naturally fall away from the fingers,** "shunning" them? A 45-degree-like angle reveals a generous, open-minded person willing to compromise and consider the options for all concerned. Ideas and concepts are important to you. You respect intelligence and individuality but are more concerned with theory rather than application. It's difficult for you to finish anything on time and are usually over budget. However, your quick-wit and humor makes you lovable and much loved.

When the **space/angle between your thumb and side of the hand is small**, hugging the fingers, you are secretive, close-minded and don't trust others easily. You reveal little about yourself, but you want to know everything about others and what makes them "tick." You have keen insight into the lives of those around you but respect intimacy and others' choices. Stubborn and willful, you like having your own way. You don't like to do things spontaneously or without adequate plotting.

A thumb with a noticeable "waist" suggests tact; the ability to understand people, animals and plants. Your boundless curiosity and desire to expand your horizons in every way is important. You seek to enhance the monotony of daily life with fantasy and entertainment. **A thick, sausage-looking thumb** reveals attitude problems and prejudice and a tendency to hurt others' feelings. Your childhood may not have been particularly enjoyable and you couldn't wait to grow up. You're not fond of the limelight and prefer working behind the scenes.

A thick and inflexible thumb can mean violence and pig-headedness. You don't expect life to be pleasant, cheery, or easy. Because you want your children or co-workers to be responsible adults, you tend to be strict and demanding. You enjoy troubleshooting and correcting errors and derive satisfaction setting things straight.

The fleshy elevation below the thumb is called the **Mount of Apollo.** Like its mythological namesake—the sun god—it speaks of personal warmth and high energy levels. When **solid, high and rounded**, you are generous, possess an enthusiasm for life and recovery quickly from illness. Self-expression is a major concern. Although you may not be great with words, you communicate rugged individuality loud and clear.

A flabby or sunken Venus-thumb area tells the poor me, self-pity soul. Emotions are confusing and you have a penchant for martyrdom, doing for others above and beyond the call of duty. You rarely heed to the here and now. Mundane day-to-day functions of the world you

FUN FACTS ABOUT PALMISTRY

It's uncertain when palmistry originated, though it was practiced in ancient
China, India, Persia, Tibet, Mesopotamia, and Egypt.

In 350 B.C., Aristotle proclaimed, "Palmistry is a judgement made of conditions, inclinations, and fortunes
of men and women, from the various lines and characters which nature imprinted in the hands."

The first known book written on palmistry was printed in 1448.

World-famous psychologist Carl Jung, an advocate of hand-examining, wrote the preface in Julius Spier's
book *Hands of Children*, singing the praises of palm-reading and uniting it to progressive psychotherapy.

Although palmistry is not grounded in traditional science, biologists acknowledge relationships between
inherited disorders such as Down's syndrome, heart defects and other maladies to palm markings.

Author Sorell writes in *The Story of the Human Hand* (1967): "We can fake and forge
the written name . . . we may change the way we sign it . . .
Our heredity rules the signs on our fingertips with authoritarian power."

Fingernails grow faster on the dominant hand. The thumb is the fastest growing nail and the little finger
is the slowest. The overall growth of human nails is 0.1 mm per day, according to age and health.

find unattractive. Beware of depression and addictive tendencies. When **extremely high and solid**, you tend to be wasteful and extravagant. You have an innate sense of drama and thrive on personal attention and satisfaction. Your mind is always racing from one thought to another and you find it difficult to concentrate.

When **flat** you are aloof, keep a distance from others. Your mind is focused on personal or internal issues rather than the outer world. No matter how good your ideas, you have difficulty explaining them to others in a logical or practical way. "Old ways" make you feel secure so you surround yourself with clones who think the way you do.

HAND LINES

Like DaVinci's etchings in the Louvre, each palm is different and carries a variation of shapes and lines. Over time, hand lines change, lengthen, or disappear. Many hands broaden or shrink in size and width. When angered or upset, hands redden; when sad or withdrawn, they turn pale.

Hands with very few lines tell of a more physical, practical, organized spirit. You love good food and sensual pleasures. You look to relationships as investments and expect a good return. **Fine thin lines** mean you are more mental and creative. You aren't much good at keeping secrets and bounce back quickly and easily from disappointments. However, too many fine or spider-webby fine lines suggest nervousness and scattered energy.

Deep, wide, well-etched lines say that you have strong feelings and specific likes and dislikes. Patient and meticulous, you're not given to storybook romance or fly-by-night schemes. You expect lovers and family to be perfect and have trouble accepting human failings or shortcomings. **Chained, feathery or broken lines** betray weak willpower, sadness, paranoia and a tendency to retreat from the physical world. You don't like being alone and are fragile in a china-doll kind of way. You might find it difficult to assert yourself or go after what you want in an aggressive, decisive way.

Long, thin hands tend to have more lines than **small or squarish hands**.

MAIN LINES

The three main lines are called the **Life** (or Vitality) **Line, the Line of Head** and **Heart Line**.

The **Life Line** doesn't reveal how long you'll live but speaks of your enthusiasm for life and willingness to enjoy and fight for what you want and love. **Deeply etched Life Lines** absent of breaks or tassels, assure a robust and fruitful life. You are a high-energy person who embraces challenge and opportunity. Affectionate and physically demonstrative, you enjoy life and people. You are known for your courage, energy, and desire to win.

Breaks and disappearances in a Life Line brand you a worrier who allows others to interfere. You are extremely jealous, possessive, and highly emo-

tional. Your relationships are punctuated with drama and emotional upheavals. Nothing comes easy.

When the **Life Line makes a wide, sweeping curve** onto a palm, you're a magnanimous, sunny individual, generous to fault (although a bit dramatic). You relate well to children and enjoy helping others in need. To you, playing weakling doesn't cut the cake. You enjoy being heard, respected, loved, and seen as strong and reliable. Generous with your time and money, you enjoy each day and want to explore new horizons and espouse new ideas.

A Life Line beginning high under the index finger area denotes a need for acknowledgment. Ego high, ambition large. The ultimate individualist, you can't bear to have someone tell you what to do or how to do it. You are combative and energetic but may have trouble disciplining yourself and focusing your abundant energy. Although you enjoy praise, it's almost impossible for you to accept advice or acknowledge errors.

When a **Life Line hugs close to the thumb**, you're not inclined to speak up and are a bit timid. More comfortable in the background than the spotlight, you enjoy helping others and are considerate of their needs, usually thinking of the greater good for the masses rather than y-o-u. Although you may be unwilling to stand up for yourself, you often fight for the rights of others. More mental than physical, you're short on vitality, requiring more rest during sickness.

THE HEAD LINE

Although your IQ or status in Mensa isn't revealed, your quality of mind and intellectual appetite is what the **Head Line** is all about. The Head Line begins on the thumb side of the hand in an area beneath the index finger and Life Line and travels across the palm towards the little finger.

Generally, a **short Head Line** that doesn't pass halfway across the palm suggests a one-track mind, short-sightedness and lack of receptivity to new ideas. You have a penchant for being orderly and are very conservative or self-centered. Issues of power and control are likely to play a role in your life. You assume authority easily and are comfortable in a decision-making role.

The longer the Head Line, the larger your scope of perception and persistence for learning. You respect knowledge, equality, and equal rights. Strongly opinionated as you are, you never tire of learning new things, enjoy companionship and probably have many friends. You may tend to overestimate yourself but your willingness to learn and quick wit takes you far. Writing, teaching, public relations or speaking would be good professions for you.

A faint or broken Head Line or one that **resembles a chain** means you're disorganized, have a wandering mind and concentrate with difficulty. You lack the organization and perseverance to see projects through to completion but are open to new ideas. You insist on being free to do things your way and tend to distance yourself from companions and co-workers.

The deeper the Head Line, the more you harness your wits and put know-how to good use. Optimistic and idealistic, you always use the silver lining inside every cloud and believe things will turn out for the better, if not the best.

If your **Head Line travels straight and level across the palm,** you're a just-the-facts cool, logical type. You prefer to talk with only those you know well and hold stubbornly to your beliefs, regardless of what others think. Mentally practical and conservative, clear thinking is your credo. Serious and, at times, pessimistic, you can become terribly critical of abstract or revolutionary ideas.

When the **Head Line** takes a **sharp upward bend towards the little finger,** you use your wits for making money—lots of it! You rarely say anything you're sorry for later. Time is money and you get things done while others dream on. This no-nonsense attitude helps you in all fields. **A Head Line curving downwards to the wrist** denotes good imagination. Lacking attention in mundane matters, you drift in and out of conversations and your mind seems always preoccupied with something else. Don't let your fantasies ride off with you.

A Head Line plummeting downward to the wrist in a sharp curve, is a sign of escapism and/or depression. Sympathetic and trusting, you are very susceptible to hard-luck stories and easily fooled. Your ego isn't exactly robust and you frequently help others at your own expense. Exercise special care with

important financial and personal decisions. Overly idealistic, living in the physical world and dealing with harsh realities are difficult for you.

When **the Head and Life Lines** join together near the thumb, you are cautious, conservative, and focused. To be happy and fulfilled on the job is your greatest source of security. Practical and predictable, your greatest gift is the structure and stability you provide to family and professionals. **A Head Line ending in a tassel-like fork**—called "a writer's fork"—shows that you're versatile, curious, and inventive. The wider the fork, the more adaptable and resourceful you are, with an ability to bring a breath of fresh air into stale, stagnant situations.

THE HEART LINE

The Heart Line is your emotional barometer and tells about your affection for people, not just lovers. It begins in an area beneath the little finger and moves across the upper portion of the palm, ending either under the base of the index, middle or ring finger.

You see your role in life as a peacemaker when possessing a **deeply etched Heart Line.** Even if you have no particular talent, you enjoy most art forms. You place great emphasis on home and family, and whether or not your experiences with family members are positive, your ties to them are strong. Because you take everything personally and want everyone to get along, you are likely to interpret differing opinions as attacks or criticisms of you. **A weak, faint line**

says that you require special attention and enjoy being pampered. Your heart rules your head, and your opinions and ideas are colored by your feelings and emotional attachments. You don't like being alone and function the best in partnerships. You want everything about your relationships to be nice all the time and can't tolerate anger or arguments.

A wide space between the Heart and Head Line says you are independent and do things your way. You approach life eagerly and aggressively and are willing to take chances that scare away cautious people. You don't enjoy slow pokes, deadbeats, or clingy people. The wider this space, the more need for freedom and individuality.

The Heart Line is considered long when it "ends" below the index finger. This is the sign of the romantic. You are protective, nurturing and devoted to friends and loved ones and don't like being alone. Not inclined to play the field, you devote much time to pursuing and maintaining relationships of all kinds. You are inclined to idealize romantic attachments and usually think the best of your partner(s).

A short Heart Line travels only halfway across the palm and says that no one takes love, sex, and

relationships more seriously than you do. Passionate and playful, sensual yet sensible, you don't leap into love affairs blindly. Once you commit yourself in love, however, you seek nothing less than a complete merger with your partner. A **chained line** or **one made up of a series of breaks** says you are fickle or inclined to change affections often. Many of your relationships are punctuated with emotional upheavals or more like romantic or casual friendships rather than deep emotional unions.

A **Heart Line travelling straight** across the palm like a ruler, rather than gently angling up or downwards, says you don't care what others think. Romance takes a backseat to a "what's-in-it-for-me?" attitude. For you, love is like a cool business deal. You can be terribly flirtatious, superficial, and self-indulgent in matters of love. A **wide space running between the Heart and Head Lines** tells of a need for independence and difficulty with emotional commitments. An individualist, you can't bear to have anyone else tell you what to do or how to do it. Highly sociable, you enjoy meeting new people and express yourself passionately, never in a roundabout way.

When the **Heart and Head Line merge** into one, also called the Simian Line, decision-making is difficult. Because your attention span is short and your interests many, you often start things but fail to finish them, you're inclined to promise more than you can deliver. Easily upset and sensitive to what you envision as personal attacks, you tend to overreact defensively when you believe you're being challenged in some way. You crave constant flattery and ego-reinforcement from friends, family, and lovers.

GIRDLE OF VENUS

Any series of U-shaped or horizontal lines between and below the middle and ring fingers and above the Heart Line constitute what is called **the Girdle of Venus**. Your sex drive is strong and you have a hearty appreciation of all physical and sensual pleasures. You have a rich fantasy mind and are keenly aware of what others think. Power is important, but you usually prefer wielding it behind the scenes. You stay on top of current events, what's hot and what's not, enjoy the arts and music and are curious about how others live. You are a bit dramatic emotionally, especially in love relationships.

FATE LINE

The **Saturn Line**, also known as the **Fate Line**, is found only 40 percent of hands and is often composed of a series of two or more vertical-running lines. It travels upwards from the wrist to the middle finger, frequently veering off course between the Head and Heart Lines and tells how you feel about the material world and economic opportunities. When clear and straight, a sense of contentment with your belongings prevails. **Broken, split or faded lines** denote dissatisfaction with status and a desire for more money and recognition is noted. Dependence on other people for

success and the need to be needed is strong when the line **curves away from the thumb**. A **double Fate Line** works best in partnerships—romantic and business— and are good at organizing others. However, a tendency to be overly cautious and skeptical often causes you to miss out on opportunities.

Many of your tests and financial hurdles involve home and family when a Saturn Line or **forked branch starts within the Life Line**. Your physical home spells security and stability to you. A traditionalist, you hold on tightly to conservative opinions: how mom or dad did it. "Old ways" make you feel secure. With this marking, inheritance or lend-lease assistance from relatives is likely

A Fate Line **ending at the Head Line** forewarns of misfortune or money loss due to poor judgement in your middle years. It's difficult for you to separate your emotions from rational thinking. It's hard for you to step outside your own needs and desires to be objective. **Stopping at the Heart Line** forewarns that business hassles are likely due to a bad choice of partners, lovers. Often your thoughts center upon what your partners or others think. Public success or recognition from peers occurs when the **Fate Line veers towards the Index Finger**.

THE VENUS LINE

Lines travelling upwards to the ring finger are called Venus Lines. One **long straight Venus line** is best, suggesting career brilliance. You can be quite charm-ing and somewhat of a flatterer when it suits your purposes. Social and very communicative, you talk to anyone who'll listen and see every conversation as an opportunity to grow and prosper. **One or two deeply etched lines that only take up the upper-half of the palm** suggest personal happiness, good imagination, and an appreciation of the arts. You comprehend the larger picture to see how all the pieces fit together and have a fantastic imagination. Your middle and later years bring success and happiness.

A **Venus line starting on the lower, thumbless side of the hand or within the Life Line and ending below the ring finger** predicts help from family. You're attentive, affectionate and loyal to those you love. However, you easily fall into ruts and routine, sacrifice your needs for others and are hesitant to take chances or change. **A multitude of Venus Lines** suggest that, although you may have your fingers in many financial pies, you will succeed on your own merits and individuality.

THE MERCURY LINE

The **Mercury Line**, also called the Hepatica, ends beneath the little finger and says how clearly you get across your point to others. Like the Fate or Saturn Line and Girdle of Venus, this line is absent in many hands. If a **series of broken or wavy lines**, hastiness, impatience and indigestion is likely. You may have trouble limiting yourself to one job, one relationship, and have several things going on simultaneously.

Your interests are many and diverse and almost anything will attract your attention for a brief time. You often promise what you can't deliver.

A series of horizontal lines leading up to the little finger reveal a hunger for learning and improved status. Although you have a high opinion of yourself, you need an audience. This demand for attention may create difficulty with close relationships. To you, more is better. **One straight clear line beginning at the wrist and ending under the little finger** says you know how to have a good time and never take life too seriously. You are optimistic and gravitate to healthy life choices and rarely allow depression, nervousness, or worry to overpower you.

AFFECTION LINES

There is a peculiar fascination about what have been called **Marriage Lines** for centuries. Twenty-first century palmistry does not acknowledge this or believe that a "legal" union can be gleaned by scanning hands—nor can the number of biological children be determined. Marriage is an institution established by the church and state and does not always reflect love or deep emotional commitment. Let's refer to these skin carvings as **Affection Lines**.

The small horizontal markings located on the inside portion of the palm lie between the base of the little finger and above the Heart Line and run parallel to the Heart Line. When one or more is **deep and well etched**, you are capable of strong, sincere affec-

tion and lasting friendship. In relationships, you are mostly concerned with permanence and security. Quality, not quantity is important to you in affairs of love. **One deep Affection Line supported by good Heart and Head Lines** equals yearning for stability and equality in relationships. You are generous and affectionate with those you care about and innately understand how to please a partner.

When these lines are **faint, chained, or broken**, you are insecure and cautious about love commitments and a bit self-critical of flaws. Traditionally, insecure in relationships, you are inclined to be overly idealistic or lazy, not doing "your part." It is difficult for you to assert yourself, go after what you want, or stand up for yourself. A good **Affection Line** should be straight and travel toward the area below the ring finger without breaks or irregular several light or broken lines reveal many fickle affairs.

When **chained or possessing a number of downward slanting lines**, there will be upset, dependency concerns, or emotional difficulties with unions. **Double or parallel lines** are said to suggest infidelity. When **no lines** are evident, relationships or marriage may be more for convenience or etiquette, not love.

It's impossible to tell precisely when love and happiness will occur but, for centuries, the general rule is that when the line is **close to the Heart Line**, you will find emotional satisfaction when young, early in life. When **close to the base of the little finger** you'll be a late bloomer.

CHAPTER FOUR

TAROT READING: IT'S IN THE CARDS

> **It would hardly be an exaggeration that the invention of the [Tarot] cards had as much impact on the thirteenth century as the invention of the novel on the eighteenth, or of radio and television on the twentieth.**
>
> —Damon Wilson, *The Mammoth Book of Nostradamus*

After I've assessed personality from handwriting, understand the client's Personal Year trends and divine tips from their palms, I address the future via the Tarot. When you do this, always remember to tie in the personal traits revealed by the previous chapter's modalities. Be considerate and grand. As Epicures said centuries ago: "It is not so much our friends' help that helps us as the confidence of their help."

The origin of the Tarot is one of history's unsolved mysteries. Forecasting probably began with the elderly—those who had lived long enough to learn that everything in life changes in cycles. Youth comes and goes, the constellations move through the sky in an orderly fashion, there are births and burials, plantings and harvests.

Observing the cyclical nature of life, the older generations knew that all setbacks were temporary, and they could encourage children with wise words like "Everything changes with time." From there, it was just a small step to realize that life cycles could be charted and correlated to more concrete, observable patterns. Stars could be watched, calendars consulted, cards read.

The 78 cards of the Tarot make up one of the tools of empowerment that have emerged throughout the centuries. Cards 0 through 21 are known as the Major Arcana. (Arcana means "profound secrets.") The rest of the deck consists of the four suits of the Minor Arcana: Cups, Pentacles, Swords, and Wands. The Tarot, like the I Ching or ancient rune stones, provides clues about your life—not answers. The cards provoke introspection. They urge you to think about your motives, and take a look at how you interact with the world.

A TAROT EXERCISE

Place yourself in a quiet room at a table with your Tarot cards. Let your mind wander for a few seconds while shuffling. Ask yourself, "What should I be aware of today?" Stop shuffling, cut the deck and examine the images of the facing card (note if reversed or upright) and consult its description.

This also works well when seeking answers to a past situation i.e., "what do I need to learn about my recent divorce?" or "what must I know about my job?"

HOW TO CONDUCT A READING

Situate yourself, or your client, in a space with no distractions. Turn on the answering machine and the telephone ringer off. Get yourself in a relaxed frame of mind; don't worry or think. Just "be." Burn a favorite incense or scented candle, play soft music. And, then:

1. Hold the deck of cards face down and shuffle through them for about fifteen seconds; take your time. Don't think about anything in particular. Keep your mind clear, open. Focus on shuffling and nothing else. (Or, if you prefer, you can concentrate on a primary concern or question. But if you keep your mind blank, the Tarot will reveal important issues for you.)

2. Using your left hand, cut the deck into four piles, placing them from left to right as shown below:

3. Take the top card from the far-left pile and turn it face up on the table in front of you. (Place it in Position A as shown.) This indicates what part of your life the reading will address. It may refer to a situation that is currently causing you concern, a problem you're trying to resolve or will soon face, an area of your life you need to work on improving, or one that will soon bring you great joy. Consider this card an outsider's view, an objective observation.

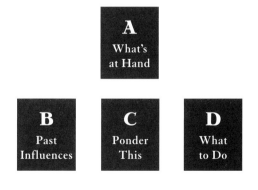

4. Take the top card from your second pile and turn it face up beneath and to the left of Card A. (Place it in Position B.) This card suggests past events, situations, and relationships that might be influencing the situation represented by Card A.

5. Place the top card from your third pile face up in Position C. This card offers food for thought, things to ponder in light of Card A.

6. Finally, turn the top card on your fourth pile face up in Position D. This card suggests answers or courses of action.

Take time to reflect on your answers. Chances are, once you've opened a line of inquiry into these issues, more ideas will reveal themselves throughout the day.

MASTERING THE TAROT

Now that you've had the opportunity to see how helpful a Tarot reading can be, you may want to add this to your fortune-telling bag of tricks. The most fluent Tarot readers know what each card signifies, and are not afraid to adjust the meaning as their intuition suggests.

To develop that kind of fluency yourself, study the following interpretations of the seventy-eight cards in the Tarot. You can refer to these until you know the cards by heart. Always bear in mind what each card's position represents, using the exercise above.

Above all, don't limit yourself to my interpretations. If the art on the cards inspires other ideas, use them. Here are a few general tips:

UPRIGHT　　　**REVERSED**

Cards fall either upright or reversed. When a card is reversed (upside down), its meaning suggests that you or your client does not feel in control of the situation. A majority of reversed cards in a layout warns against laziness and depending too much on others; it often signifies "no" to a yes-or-no query. A majority of upright cards suggests control, or a good time for action; or a "yes" concerning a yes-or-no query.

Note which group of cards is dominant in a reading. Several Major Arcana cards signal that you are serious about the matter/decision. Note the majority of Minor Arcanum. For instance, a majority of Cups warns against letting feelings cloud reason. Lots of Swords forewarn indecision on your part. Wands say "act now." Pentacles urge you or your client to approach everything like an accountant. In other words, aim for balance, profit.

THE SUITS

THE MAJOR ARCANA

The Major Arcana cards represent major lessons to be mastered on the road of life. These cards symbolize human life—physical, intellectual, emotional, and spiritual. Explore your strengths and weaknesses, hopes and fears—the deepest part of your personality.

THE SUIT OF CUPS

The Suit of Cups is one of emotions, relationships, and the unconscious. Upright Cup cards in a layout reveal that feelings are extremely sensitive, quickly engaged and easily hurt. Many reversed Cups warn against being detached, too cool, callus.

THE SUIT OF PENTACLES OR "COINS"

Money makes the world go 'round. The suit of Coins represents the Almighty Buck, work, career, everything material, real and solid. These cards are concerned with the mundane aspects of life, how you get things done, your reality—things you can touch, taste, smell and measure in order to comprehend them. When Coin cards fall in upright positions, you're in more control and less likely to be duped by anyone stronger. Reversed—Coin cards suggest confusion or intimidation about material/physical concerns.

THE SUIT OF SWORDS

Modern swords are helpful kitchen utensils that can double as dangerous weapons. They cut two ways. Sometimes they represent breakthroughs in communication; other times, breakdowns. Problems are troubles, stress and worries are attributed to the Swords. When they fall in upright positions, you're likely to be victorious. Confusion and a need to look objectively are indicated when Swords lay reversed, upside-down.

THE SUIT OF WANDS

Action, enthusiasm, passion, zeal, personal enterprise, and health are keywords for the suit of Wands. When they fall upright in a layout you're in the driver's seat; when reversed, the steering wheel is in another's hands.

MAJOR ARCANA

0. THE FOOL

Take things as they are; don't fret or be critical. Timing may seem off, but matters are proceeding as expected, planned. Do your part to settle disagreements. Kill others with kindness and let them sleep in their own bed. If you must take chances or do something that you can't foresee the outcome, this is as good a time as any. Good time to improve investments and the home.

Reversed—Schedules are full, time is at a premium. Conflicting opinions may confuse. Don't get shook or act bullheaded! Take time to enjoy life's pleasures. Postpone decisions for the moment. Use discretion and patience. The more carefully you perform any task, the more chance it will succeed now. Your instincts are working well, so trust them!

1. THE MAGICIAN

Don't cross swords or worry. Stretch yourself, "push the envelope," test your limits. Success, recognition come as a result of being adventurous, aggressive, daring, competitive, and using wisdom. Delegate and discard. The occasions when your own needs coincide with your partners and loved ones seem to be few and far between at the moment. You know that you can get where you want to go. Your strength lies in not letting others upset you.

Reversed—Remain committed to the course of action that feels right to you. Stay aware of rules and tradition and think twice before acting. Don't close yourself off from outside help or guidance and beware of arrogance. Don't disregard others or be abrasive. Beware of obstacles. You simply cannot afford to anger or antagonize the wrong people now. Make friends, not enemies.

2. THE HIGH PRIESTESS

Listen to intuition rather than analysis, feelings instead of facts. Be mindful of shared confidences. Take time to meditate about options, what's best for you. Learn from the difficulties and "tests" of the real world. To be a winner: don't withdraw. Ask what is holding you back from achieving a long-term ambition. Try not to fall out with friends who truly have your interests at heart.

Reversed—Laziness, lack of focus. You want things to come easily and may give up too quickly, rather than work diligently toward goals. A desire to escape, withdraw into yourself increases. Beware of drugs, alcohol. Not a good time to confront your partner with any problems in your relationship.

3. THE EMPRESS

Express your ideas, take calculated risks. Take responsibility to get what you want. Passion, doing what comes naturally, nurturing others takes center stage. Discern between love and lust. A good time to negotiate any difficult or contentious matters rather than sweep them under the carpet. News of wedding, pregnancy, children arrives.

Reversed—Are you feeling inferior concerning your intellect, education or communication skills? If so, stop! If you act unconsciously or blindly, you are likely to fail. Don't exaggerate fears, or be reluctant to take action. A line must be drawn between what is possible and what is not. Extravagance and the desire for beautiful things increase. Problems with mother or close females are likely.

4. THE EMPEROR

An energetic time when you can assert yourself effectively and accomplish a great deal of work. Success depends upon how well you express yourself. Play by the rules, don't cut corners or shortcut how things are supposed to be. Use common sense when managing resources. It's time to organize, plan. Logic and reason delivers excellent results.

Reversed—Despite your obvious capabilities, success comes slow at this time. Respect the past and learn from it; accept favors from others. Frustrations, obstacles, delays or setbacks test your perseverance. Take the impersonal, unemotional route. Balance work with play.

5. THE HIEROPHANT

Seek the tried-and-true path, remain conventional at this time. Your public image, your status in your circle of friends and community are of great concern. Don't sacrifice personal beliefs or freedoms, but remain alert to the outside world. Don't let anyone's doubts deter you from embarking on a potentially rewarding enterprise.

Reversed—Make things happen by taking care of details. Don't become so rigidly attached to order and routine that the ritual means more than the result. Personal growth comes from modesty and compassion. Don't let superstition scare you. Anger and irritability on the rise, more accident-prone than ever now.

6. THE LOVERS

Romantic unions, close friends, home life improve. Take time for lovemaking, telling those closest to you what they mean to you. Examine relationships that are going nowhere; eliminate unwanted, unnecessary people. Be kind to others. Not a good time for career change. Don't force issues.

Reversed—Exaggeration abounds, emotions on the increase; jealousy, envy is on the rise. Romantic unions are tested, separation likely. Slow down and refuse to let anyone rush you or push you into anything. Beware of self-indulgence, greed, and power plays. Speak up; be willing to roll with punches. A good time to demonstrate to others that you can work on your own and do it well.

7. THE CHARIOT

Good time for travel, getting away. Show others your backbone, be strong. Victory is on the horizon! Reject negative people but don't judge harshly. You now have the ability to make things happen. Good luck for students, writers. Appeal to other's sense of fair play; reject negative types. When it comes to career or health, you may want to get a second opinion.

Reversed—People are more defensive so don't give in to intimidation, pressure. Roll up your sleeves and give it all you've got: no one wants to waste time now. Travel goes poorly now. Expect delays, last-minute cancellations of plans. You may be left to fend for yourself for awhile, since most others in your orbit are apt to be busy with their own problems.

8. JUSTICE

What you see is what you get; what goes around arrives. Seek legal counsel, ask advice from elders. Good luck with negotiations, government agencies. Unless you can do healthy things, what's right and just, be prepared to pay the piper.

Reversed—Tell the truth or get ready to suffer the consequences. Others are wishy-washy now. Do your part to say what's real and what you feel. Let go of the past and resolve to turn over a new leaf, seek another approach.

9. THE HERMIT

Break an unnecessary habit, get rid of "friends," circumstances that drive you crazy. Take steps to eliminate yourself from unhealthy ruts, routine. Don't let anyone talk you out of doing what you know is right. Refuse to get stuck in other's expectations. Take time for yourself; meditate on what's important and real.

Reversed—Don't let responsibilities, superficial actions weigh you down. Spend time with one you love; take care of unfinished business. Beware of what's going on around you; seek advice but don't be a sucker for a sob story. Be open, forthright. Beware of self-pity. You are in a strong position to tackle a dilemma at home or work, but you still need to discern a certain someone's agenda.

10. WHEEL OF FORTUNE

You made your bed, now sleep in it! Own up to your actions, responsibilities or suffer the consequences. Be true to yourself. Good time for personal getaway. Show others your backbone and personal strength. Clean out your address book; try someone/something new. Clinging to the old slows down the process of embracing the new.

Reversed—Luck isn't on your side now. Put up or shut up. Don't get embroiled in anything you'll regret; be constructively selfish. Not a time to be alone. Experiment. Someone close is determined to call the shots. Before you start asking questions, be sure that you want to know the answers.

11. STRENGTH

Deny pettiness and prejudice; make peace not enemies. Weigh out all sides of situations. Long-buried tensions resurface and demand to be handled. Refuse to be so set in your ways that you miss the "big picture." Ego and stubbornness on the rise. Clear the air as quickly as you can. Be careful to examine all the cards in your hand before showing them.

Reversed—Everyone expects the best from you, and, vice versa. Don't give in to intimidation or pressure, or go to bed angry. Are you seeing things realistically? Arguments between lovers, close associates are likely. Unpleasant as it may be to deal with someone who is being difficult, you will learn a great deal about yourself in the process. Wait for another day to take action.

12. THE HANGED MAN

Rise above material concerns, how things "should" have been. Try another avenue. Matters slow down, are stifled now. Relax and re-groove. Keep everything aboveboard, and allow others to change their mind, opinions. Contemplate, don't agitate. Let the evidence speak for itself.

Reversed—Stop being so close-minded. There are plenty of alternatives to your problems. Try something new. Keep everything above board and carry the elbow grease. Not a time to be lazy, melancholy. Your general rashness/ignorance can lead to an accident; be careful of injuries to the head.

13. DEATH

A growth phase. Acknowledgment comes slow; no one will pitch in unless you beg. Don't take "no" as final or brood about the past. Refuse to buy into self-pity, laziness, old habits. Stop doing what's not "right"! Be careful about falling into childish behavior patterns. You must be very conscious of what you're doing at this time.

Reversed—Be prepared to lend a shoulder and a handkerchief. A romantic or creative proposition may not be all that it seems—don't overcommit yourself until you know the whole story. Ask for a favor, and give one too. Temporary setbacks, delays are likely. Great time for healthy escapism. Honesty brings rewards.

14. TEMPERANCE

Try to see the other side of the story. The middle path wins. Use common sense, good management. Others are more clannish, set in their ways now. Postpone arguments, debates. Compromise delivers happiness. If you have to convince someone of a point of view or sell him or her something, you should be very effective, as long as you can avoid high-pressuring them.

Reversed—Others play to win now; don't be foolish, self-centered. But don't believe all you hear. Lots of ego-posturing in the air. Your sense of judgement is impaired; relax. Accept favors, be kind but listen to your Higher Self. Let bygones be. Good time for reunions, nostalgia. Phone home, make peace.

15. THE DEVIL

Desire dominates, matter overpowers mind. Beware of your dark side. Materialistic pleasures taints clear-thinking now. Discern who's "addicted" to what; cleanse yourself of unhealthy behavior. If a business partner or someone near and dear is behaving out of character, chances are it's a reaction to something that has placed you in a bad light. Be strong; don't be a fool!

Reversed—Things are unclear now. Refuse to be intimidated and don't judge others too harshly. Refuse to let past issues cloud today's progress. Others are uptight, set in their ways. (Are you?) Clear the air as quickly as you can, restores relationships to normal footing.

16. THE TOWER

Whether or not you feel irritable, and you very likely will, today may be full of disputes and arguments unless you try to understand other people's points of view. Everyone wants to be admired now. Bottom-lines, what's necessary and real prevails; illusions get shattered, enemies revealed. Others embellish the truth. Don't get cranky if situations don't come out as planned. Count to ten before acting.

Reversed—Delays are inevitable; a fall from glory likely. Rest up; take a break. Release old ties. Avoid rash, impulsive actions. Your ego energies are high, but in such a way that you're likely to assert yourself inappropriately. Be prepared to change plans in midstream. Cooperation is minimal, pushiness is plentiful now. Meet opposition with sympathy and compassion.

17. THE STAR

If you have high expectations of yourself, there's nothing you can't accomplish now—you only have to put a name to your dream for it to come true. Stay awake and pace yourself! If you nod off or get lazy, you may miss it. This is the card of optimism and hope. You have a chance to start over in long-standing situations. Be a star, but beware of pride; aim for cooperation and innovation, not ego.

Reversed—Remain humble. Even though you feel like a puppet on a string, you're not as powerless as you think. You need imagination to come up with options for action now. Examine and evaluate carefully. There are a number of small but important things you've been neglecting. Catch up on them. Try not to view everyone as rivals because a great many people are on your side.

18. THE MOON

People are clannish, set in their ways, full of emotions. Don't join the crowd, and read between the lines. Intuition is high, but deception is likely. People feel like staying to themselves. Not the time to start anew. Have patience.

Reversed—Everyone wants things done their way, so go easy on yourself. Take a "sick day" from responsibilities, roll with punches. Get away from day-to-day routine. Don't be too trusting, over willing to go that extra mile unless you want to (or can afford it).

19. THE SUN

Your growth and personal expansion are linked to self-expression now. Intuition is on the increase. Say what you feel when you feel it. Accept criticism, admit mistakes. You have a strong tendency to regard all issues as serious if they involve your pride. Be careful in your evaluations. Enthusiasm brings results. A promotion, improved love life is on the horizon.

Reversed—Relationship hassles are likely now. Don't get wrapped up in yourself so tightly that you ignore other's needs. Stop being overly dramatic. Aim for the realistic, what's good for all concerned parties. Don't take unnecessary risks, and avoid situations that might weaken your body and make you susceptible to illness.

20. JUDGEMENT

A job well done delivers rewards; laziness is punished. Make peace, don't nit-pick or judge yourself or others too harshly. Patience brings just desserts. Don't be cruel. Health improves (but it may take some effort on your part). Don't worry. What emerges is more productive and rewarding in the long run.

Reversed—The desire to escape, let others take control is high. Self-esteem is low and needs a boost. Keep your ears open but your mouth closed. Read all fine print. Act, don't fear—shift into fast gear! As long as you're prepared to do your part, no obstacle is insurmountable.

21. THE WORLD

Avoid focusing on what went wrong or turned sour. What others say belongs to them—go with the flow! You are free to follow the dictates of your heart. Refuse to get shaken if others undermine your confidence. Don't give up anything for anyone.

Reversed—Don't be overly trusting or willing to believe what others say. Foolishly overestimating your abilities may cause you to bite off more than you can chew; stay within your own limits. Pamper yourself and the object of your affection. Seek intimacy, personal happiness. Conclusions come slow, but are worthwhile.

SUIT OF CUPS

ACE OF CUPS

Happiness arrives soon but may take some effort and elbow grease to make it manifest. Those around you are more emotional, clannish. Postpone debates at this time; listen to your intuition but don't expect bottom-line answers. Examine home, family issues. A good time for renovating, relocating. When dealing with both intensely personal and professional issues try to remember that fear is only an illusion: something that gives a false sense of isolation that exists only in the imagination.

Reversed—Be willing to accept favors, assistance; don't be selfish, too full of yourself. Act with determination, break an unnecessary habit, know when to say "no." In spite of the challenges, conflicts and divided loyalties know that you must cherish both the coming together and the going apart to know love, contentment, and fulfillment. When you meet opposition with self-confidence, you will succeed.

TWO OF CUPS

New friends help decision-making. Good time to make peace with anyone who's recently done you wrong. Expect a happy surprise, love letter, new relationship. Now you are in the position to ring in as many changes as you deem necessary. You can finally turn the tables on rivals, competitors or mischief-makers. Refuse to buy into social intimidation.

Reversed—Don't be insensitive; keep things light! Good time to apologize, kiss and make up. Refuse to let anyone or anything raise your blood pressure. Others may be asking too much of you now, needing to cry on your shoulder. Avoid arguments with kith and kin and be prepared for travel plans to be delayed or cancelled. Constructive outlets to relieve tension are best.

THREE OF CUPS

Overspending comes easy now, so watch it! Others want hugs, acknowledgment, your undivided attention; beware of bluntness or callous feelings. Flexibility and adaptability bring luck. Reject negative types and refuse to get discouraged. Family problems begin to mellow. Now's the time when no one and nothing can prevent you from charting your own course and choosing your very own travelling companion.

Reversed—Don't let disappointments get in the way of happiness. Beware of overindulgence, depression. Tendency to overdo, act on illusion. Jealousy clouds reason, logic; don't be impressed by what "the Jounces" have. Luck from young women arrives. Stay near homebase and keep things safe. There is always a certain amount of turmoil—and it would seem that many of life's lessons are learned through trial and error now.

FOUR OF CUPS

Take a step back and look at matters from a different perspective. The heart rules the head. Share your thoughts and gains, don't be selfish. Do your part to settle disagreements. Be a grown-up. Confrontations set you free now.

Reversed—Dishonesty is not in your nature, so avoid involvement with anyone who has something to hide. With so much going on beneath the surface now, you are hardly in your element. Power plays are on the rise. Don't jump the gun or get angry when others disagree. Hurt feelings could keep you from taking the best course of action. Be open for new friendships, relationships, but watch finances!

FIVE OF CUPS

Keep your emotions in check at this time, beware of deception, illusion. Reinforce your beliefs with facts and demand the same from others. Take care of unfinished business. Do your part to settle disagreements. Good time for bodywork, surgery, making babies. remain true to your principles and ideals.

Reversed—Friends bring support, assistance. Good time for vacation, getting away from the daily grind. Don't let yourself get overburdened with chores, responsibilities. Rise above pettiness, prejudice. It's time to relax and replenish yourself. The pace is hectic now, so slow down and count your true blessings. Don't compromise your integrity for the sake of others' peace of mind while ignoring your own.

SIX OF CUPS

Your potential for change has never been better, but it's up to you to transform your life now. Be firm with affairs of the heart. Amid current emotionalism, be flexible, spontaneous and loose. Personal magnetism increases. Don't let the past distract from the present. Good time for love affairs, renewing vows. Invest in your home space.

Reversed—Make good all promises and refuse to buy into intimidation, demands from others. Refuse to get pushed around and refrain from being pushy. Be constructive, not cranky. Make time for belly laughs, new friends. It's not a productive period when you 'see' results. However, now's the time when the handwriting on the wall-of-dreams is more easily understood.

SEVEN OF CUPS

Act kindly and calmly, don't loose your cool. A good time for reevaluating matters, getting plans in motion. Call an old lover and tell them you're a better person for knowing them. Truth is soon revealed. Not everything attempted can be achieved; therefore, you must stop feeling guilty about falling short of your high standards.

Reversed—Plan for the future instead of living in the past. Make sure you're speaking clearly; emotions are high and mighty. Beware of over doing things, falling into excess, feeling sorry for you. Patience factors are low. Provide reassurance to loved ones. Remain relaxed. Double-check medications, re-examine health regime.

EIGHT OF CUPS

Extravagance and self-sacrifice rears its head now. Beware of quarrels, disputes; use caution in love affairs, affections. Attention spans are short, so don't take things too personal. Changed circumstances mean changed priorities, so don't be afraid to reconsider a decision. Since others seem to be thinking along innovative lines, you have nothing to lose by joining them. Count your blessings and be content for what happens.

Reversed—Emotions run high; aim for less pressure and more light heartedness. Let go of situations that no longer concern you. Spend some time and money on what makes you feel good. Good news arrives through the mail, when at home. What occurs now helps you understand the reasons behind loved one's behavior. Not a time to be deprived or melancholy. Wake up, baby!

NINE OF CUPS

A chance to improve your financial and romantic interests soon means that you must look at your future in terms of past experience. People are generous to those in need. Stroke others' egos and razzle-dazzle them with everything you've got. Refrain from shoptalk, worrying about finances. Just reevaluate and enjoy the kindness of strangers.

Reversed—Your thoughts may be far away, but the business of life lies close ahead. Considerable gains are on the horizon. Postpone decision-making; weigh options. Emotions are on the rise. Let others whine or bark and get on with your life. No one minces words now; beware of arrogance. Be footloose, not uptight. A wish soon comes true.

TEN OF CUPS

Tender words and sympathy brings best results. Speak from your heart. A sudden love affair or flirtation is likely. Food and drink become more attractive now, so beware of overdoing it. Leave the answering machine on and let someone else get the door. Your ability to cut through superficial details and get to the root of your difficulties proves invaluable.

Reversed—Don't look a gift horse in the mouth. Be kind to strangers, as well as yourself. Emotions are uncentered; be discreet, follow through on promises. Your achievements will be determined by your resources and if your resources don't stretch as far as you would like, then now is the time to boost your earning power! Be alert to financial obligations; pay taxes, loans, repay favors.

QUEEN OF CUPS

People are more set in their ways now. Life is more than your day-to-day job, worries. Make time to examine spiritual beliefs, higher thought. Don't get bogged down in trivial details or the demands of others. Help from older women arrive soon. Tangible results may be few and far between at the moment, but at least you can start laying the foundations for a more secure and satisfying way of life.

Reversed—Let others have their way now. Others are more businesslike, stuffy. Even if you hate to say you're sorry, you'll find it easy to beg for forgiveness or ask a favor now. Be cautious in your spending and aware of what you truly need. Take time to rethink matters, eating patterns. Go shopping for new clothes and home items. Celebrate life!

KING OF CUPS

Be happy for what happens today; go easy on yourself. Control your temper and don't take criticism too personally. No matter how ambitious you happen to be, you're about to discover that there are more important things than "things" or fame. True happiness comes from doing what feels right and makes the world a better place. Work with time, don't let time work you over.

Reversed—People will plod along slowly now; keep a backup plan handy. Exaggeration is in the stars, so read between the lines. Don't give away too much of yourself or you could wind up short. Make amends and move on. Good time for rest, recuperation, and assistance from older friends, family.

PAGE OF CUPS

Don't get upset if things aren't going as you hoped; be open to alternatives. Be prepared to change plans in midstream. Beware of childish behavior, ignorance. Think before reacting. Let family and friends have their own way, even if you don't agree with what they're doing. Don't play games.

Reversed—A good time for independent action, going your own way. Friends, coworkers may not understand your feelings so you're on your own now! Don't let emotions overpower you or judge others too harshly. If it feels as if loved ones or influential associates are working against you, it is only because you have conflicting agendas with them. Patience wins.

KNIGHT OF CUPS

Look at situations as just another challenge. You will not only overcome it, you will be in a position to win the day! Let others pamper you; do something nice for yourself. Being depressed or playing meanie won't cut the cake. Control your temper and refuse to be intimated by loud or pushy people. No matter how argumentative others may be, you must stick up for your personal ideals.

Reversed—The obvious solution may not be the right one; weigh out matters. Don't be in a hurry to get things done; stop and think things out before acting. Blow kisses, not money. Good time for a vacation, playing hooky from responsibilities. Don't try to cut corners or ignore the facts when plain-speaking and honesty will get you further.

SUIT OF PENTACLES OR "COINS"

ACE OF COINS

You want to get things done and don't take chances with your money or time. Economy, simplicity bring rewards now. This card heralds good luck with new business endeavors and acknowledgment for a job well done. Apply for new work, seek a promotion. Don't hide your light under a bushel basket—reveal your radiance. Enjoy—and demand—life's pleasures: simple, and otherwise.

Reversed—Are you appreciating what you have, own, believe to be yours? Don't let self-doubt get the best of you or squelch your intentions, goals. Money is tight now, budgeting is a necessity. Beware of reckless, irresponsible people. Surround yourself with colleagues looking out for your best interests. Be willing to try your hand at something new. Last year's debits are last winter's snowflakes: old, cold. Hotter times are ahead.

TWO OF COINS

It is difficult for you to determine what has greater priority now: your needs or other people's. Improved working relationships are just around the corner. Let go of something old in preparation for new opportunities. Keep your ears tuned to alternative business proposals. Brainstorm with peers; teamwork works. Help is on its way. Explore teamwork.

Reversed—Reflect carefully about your motives for dealing with people. If your integrity is high, you won't have to worry that your achievements may someday fall apart to make way for something better. Take care not to undermine your own financial stability in the process.

THREE OF COINS

You have an overwhelming desire to do good work now—and you will! Get involved in other's affairs: family, employers. Use your know how to help them as well as yourself. Trying to people-please or "buy" anybody with gifts will only lead to resentment. Now you can be as silver-tongued as anyone can when it suits you, and charm birds off the trees.

Reversed—Because of your generosity—or insecurities—you may feel overly generous to those in need, thereby diminishing your financial balance as well as physical energies—the only result will be a significant reduction in both. Beware of unemployment; do what's expected. Plan ahead; be willing to make certain sacrifices. Good time for job interviewing.

FOUR OF COINS

When managing financial affairs, be careful that you don't lose perspective on ethical standards. Respect those in power but don't feel intimidated by anyone who seems to have more clout or strength. Although your ideas are rich, they may still need to be developed to be useful. Meditate, seek balance. Good time for business partnerships, beginning new financial endeavors.

Reversed—The demands of personal security weighs mightily on your shoulders now. Confusion and a sense of loss are likely if you let greed or insecurity take over. Challenge and opposition are on the horizon. The world doesn't owe you anything: contribute to your personal causes and show others your true worth.

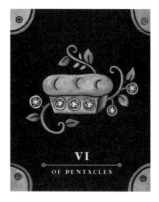

FIVE OF COINS

Although you extend yourself through effort and hard work, recent demands may have forced you to concede to working with and for others. Let them know what you expect. Your greatest challenge comes from comparing what you get for your personal services with what others get from theirs. Beware of weak vitality and financial problems at this time.

Reversed—It goes against your grain when associates suggest you should adhere to a particular code of behavior. Learning the virtues of self-discipline and contribution brings substantial rewards. Reserve the right to express yourself as freely as you choose. Be ethical and relaxed. A new source of income, or loans repaid, is likely.

SIX OF COINS

Benefits soon arrive thanks to the amount of effort you've recently put out. Keep money matters in perspective, and stop being overly sensitive to the needs of others in job demands. Your fantasies may be spilling over into the real world, so be extra careful to avoid more liabilities than assets. Beware of overindulgence and too much of a "good thing." Weight gain comes easy now.

Reversed—Don't feel insecure by working too hard or going too far beyond the call of duty. Choose well-defined objectives that provide growth for you and yours but beware of bribery at this time. Slowing down improves your well being. Unless all else fails, don't borrow now because becoming obligated will take the starch out of your sails.

SEVEN OF COINS

Have you been jumping the gun lately? Hard work and patience promises rewards. Listen to others and postpone decisions until you are thoroughly informed. Because you hate to be cash-shy, you may take on more responsibilities than you can handle. Loans get repaid now. Go easy on yourself.

Reversed—Even though you may like the final word, there's no harm in asking for advice. Take time to be thoroughly informed, don't jump the gun. Roll up your sleeves and bring out the elbow grease! Teamwork and assistance is on the horizon when you ask. Don't ignore the rules of the game or simply trust luck.

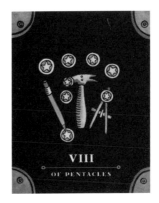

EIGHT OF COINS

Don't assume you know it all or that the world twirls around your schedule. You want the best for your loved ones but must be willing to roll with the punches. Your strength can uplift those who lack the resources to handle it alone. You have lots to learn. When you lack information, have the belief in yourself and the determination to find it.

Reversed—People to turn to you when needed; good time for accepting favors, assistance. Don't be a solo act. Get off your high horse and be a willing listener. Expect temporary delays, postponements concerning leases, loans. You're only shortchanging yourself if you are looking only for instant financial benefits.

NINE OF COINS

Though you have always been available to those who need your assistance, seek new outlets, information and resources. The time for benefits, paybacks, rewards is quickly approaching—but only if you're sincere and work diligently. No pain, no gain. Now's your time to manifest your heart's desire.

Reversed—Plan carefully what for whatever you hope to achieve now, without assuming everything will work out as expected. Don't be afraid to ask for help. Don't embroider your ideals or opinions onto other's desires. Concentrate on the greater Good for all. Don't overtax your strength or health.

TEN OF COINS

At this time, your creative imagination is second to none. Express yourself—your services are finally in demand! When you reach one goal, another will present itself. Guilt about presumed inadequacies can lead to health problems now. Be prudent and confident. Plan now, refuse to be deterred from your goals. Luck comes from the elderly.

Reversed—The problems of the "real world" may now require that you relieve others' burdens. Just remember to keep personal goals foremost in your mind. Friends show their true colors, so eliminate anyone who doesn't believe in you. Be on the lookout for legal entanglements, snafus at this time. What you feel and believe is worth more than what you earn and own.

QUEEN OF COINS

Carry out your plans, don't doubt your ability to live up to responsibilities or ignore your feelings—believe in yourself but don't expect approval at this time. Things are tough now. Rewards arrive when you work on your own, in your own fashion. Refuse to make promises you can't deliver. Quiet-time is minimal, so make due. There is a limit to even how many loads you can carry.

Reversed—Those around you are acting stuffier than normal. Pay no attention. Take time to rethink matters, especially your eating habits.

KING OF COINS

Be a specialist rather than a Jack-or-Jill-of-all trades now. You have strong sensual and physical desires now but the disciplinarian in you may interfere with personal happiness. Rise above material and emotional insecurities, mobilize your resources. You know how difficult it would be to lose everything you've worked so hard for. Applause from authority figures arrives.

Reversed—You're extremely sensitive now, more vulnerable to people's suggestions. Chill out and wear a secret smile! Fear of competition will delay desired outcome. Act, don't pout. By avoiding confrontation, you'll miss an opportunity to learn how to effectively deal with challenges. Tell partners your objectives, what you feel. Don't be afraid of rejection.

PAGE OF COINS

You now attract cues for your goals from people you admire. You've been pretty good about demonstrating your people skills, lately. Haven't you? Since you want to be financially independent, start now! You may have to put up with recent criticism from friends or family recently, but now's the time to push forward and improve your quality of life! Luck comes from young females.

Reversed—You're a pal, a friend in need, always there. Although circumstances may have shaken your foundations recently, stop being hesitant or doubting that you'll succeed. Don't underestimate your earning capacities. Fear of competition only wastes time you can use to meet it successfully. Not a good time for travel.

KNIGHT OF COINS

You're questioning whether or not you'll have enough money to get everything you want, right? Be content with what you have. You rarely get discouraged but, lately, your greatest liability is lack of restraint in spending. Success is around the corner, but until you learn to budget time and money, it will take its time.

Reversed—You're badly in need of a less stressful lifestyle. In order to fit into the social environment you aspire to, you're going to have to stop overspending. Cut back. Review who owes what to whom. Home improvement projects flourish now. Your goals may seem distant, but they are worth pursuing. Don't put them off!

SUIT OF SWORDS

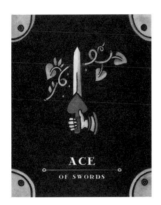

ACE OF SWORDS

Your aggressive, pioneering spirit is strong, but don't let your ego get in the way. Push ahead with ideas, contract negotiation, legal matters. Use reason and logic; refuse to let your heart rule your head. Goals you can achieve quickly are better for you than ones that require years of planning. Take things at a slower pace. Don't go too far out on a limb.

Reversed—Things are out of balance; use patience and perseverance. A good time for solo work, acting independently. Don't distort facts or act abrasively. You need a cooling off period; inform associates how much is at stake and what must be preserved. Avoid focusing on what went wrong; you are free to follow the dictates of your heart.

TWO OF SWORDS

Refusing to face problems will only increase their potency. Don't nurse too many pains. Matters begin to mellow; help is on the way. A slowing down, rose-smelling time. Lend a shoulder but not your money. Don't scatter your energies or spread yourself too thin. Carefully planned activity brings success. Intuition is foggy now; think twice.

Reversed—Your inability to see merit in all sides of matters causes difficulty. You're not inclined to think in group terms now; you don't want to waste time trying to relate to others. Be open to suggestions; don't delude yourself into thinking you have to control everything. Beware of people who don't have your best interests in mind. Aim for cooperation, not confrontation.

THREE OF SWORDS

The "divorce" card: beware of misinterpreting other's intentions. This may be a time of regret or separation, so keep your chin up and look for the light at the end of the tunnel. Don't let nervousness or worry cloud clear thinking and action. Conflicts are likely in your domestic or professional life or any area in which your ego is intimately involved. While it is necessary to assert yourself, don't overdo it! Take a break, get some rest.

Reversed—This is a good time to make reforms in your life and to become more effective in changing the world around you. But don't rebel or fall into denial against "what is." Situations become sluggish, postponements are inevitable. Are you looking at things honestly? How can you get behind the steering wheel and get back in control? Proceed forward and roll with all punches.

FOUR OF SWORDS

Opposition lessens; help arrives. Be sure that you haven't left any loose ends in what you have been doing up until now. Avoid temptation; don't act ruthlessly. Try a conservative, middle of the road approach to soothe disagreements, arguments. Depending on how badly you may want to do something, you will either fight for it harder or give up altogether. The greatest obstacle to your success is impatience.

Reversed—Keep things simple, delegate, and, for once, allow others to do most of the fetching and carrying. In some way, you are likely to experience difficulties in the area of communication. Let associates lend a hand, don't get stuck in nostalgia, the past. Family friends and associates supply answers soon. Luck arrives concerning past legal concerns—but be sure to read the fine print!

FIVE OF SWORDS

Have your hopes been broken, are your spirits down? Are you overwhelmed? It's now time for rest and re-prioritizing. Beware of theft or letting others take advantage of you. Keep up your spirits and polish your armor. Don't get hung up on opposition, dead ends. It is important to be still and listen to your inner voice, which is now telling you that even a financial or emotional setback has only set you free. You're not as powerless as you may feel.

Reversed—Accept negative experiences without blame—out of humility comes serenity. Beware of pessimism, low self-esteem. Although you may have to work harder and success may not come quickly, situations soon begin to turn around. Structured, impersonal, unemotional environments provide assistance. Don't neglect your diet, health concerns. Until situations blow over, allow yourself playtime.

SIX OF SWORDS

Formulate objectives for long-range efforts. Find out what you want to change about yourself and your world and get to work on those changes! To achieve security and happiness, you must plan your future goals carefully now. Know when to say "no" and maintain your integrity. Take time for yourself, play hooky, take a vacation. Faraway friends and outsiders provide remedies.

Reversed—Competition is the key to your greatest accomplishments. Learn from opposition. Take a step back, use your peripheral vision and look outside yourself for alternatives. Solutions manifest when getting away from day-to-day duties, doldrums. Good time for taking a trip over water, beach vacation. What is really needed is a cooling-off period and for everyone to realize how much is at stake and what must be persevered.

SEVEN OF SWORDS

Get everything in writing. Trust yourself, don't let associates inhibit your needs, goals. Plans are problematic, friends may let you down. Your greatest mistake is failing to cultivate your creative talents, relying too much on others, being too trusting. Long-term assets count for more than transient pleasures now. Let go, take a risk. You cannot lose what's not yours to begin with.

Reversed—Who are your true friends? Who do you really trust? Pressure is on the rise to deliver what other's want. Refuse to bite off more than you can chew. Don't be overly impressed by competitors. Learn from other's successes and failures. There is more than one way of looking at a problem—especially in relation to a personal or romantic affair.

EIGHT OF SWORDS

Roll with all punches when you hear gossip or encounter opposition from those who are set in their ways. Postpone ultimatums, "bottom lines," and don't take everything as "fact." Update your resume, be open to new business deals. Think about your financial needs and tomorrows. Good financial news arrives soon via e-mail or post. Accept different ways to reach your goals.

Reversed—Don't get intimidated or overly eager for instant results. This is a slowing down period that delivers freedom from what's been restricting happiness and peace of mind. Don't be close-minded or petty. Cool it. Circumstances have not been easy recently. More than anything, you need some tender loving care. Be sure you know where a relationship is heading before making serious plans.

NINE OF SWORDS

Rid yourself of hangers-on and those who're cruel or critical of you. Depression, suspicion, or self-doubt takes the spotlight now, so read between the lines and don't lose focus. Don't be a victim of intimidation or other's greed. Quarrels, despondency likely—let go of the negative, unconstructive. Therapy, meditation goes well. Make good use of private, quiet time.

Reversed—Confusion, poor decision-making rules. Expectations falter due to naivete. Refuse to use manipulative or unscrupulous tactics to get what you think is necessary. Use intuition as your guide. No one is trying to block your progress or hamper your happiness; it's just that they need to know exactly what to do. Knowing where you're heading is half the battle.

TEN OF SWORDS

Ten of Swords—Don't be content with moderate gains or settling for second best. Accept setbacks and take on competitors. Troubles in personal relationships are building, weighing on your mind. Your ability to solve problems can be determined only when you apply what you know and feel. Don't rush into anything that needs to simmer gently before coming to a boil. Don't feel pinned down.

Reserved—Mental focus is unclear. Beware of back problems, taking on too much. Someone you love or respect will soon give you the stimulus you need to exploit your talents. When you resolve self-doubt and fear, you will gain proof of your capabilities. Setbacks and reversals are normal for people pursuing an objective. Go easy on yourself.

QUEEN OF SWORDS

Beware of those who only have their own best interest at hand. You're likely to be victimized by someone shrewder or cleverer now. Let others make their own bed and sleep in it. Be on the lookout for dishonesty. Be your own person. You'll soon be in a position to share your load. Time heals all wounds.

Reversed—Time to get back up on your feet, bark louder, do your own thing. You're on your own for moment, so get comfortable. Heavy demands are creating doubt; don't worry or feel deserted. Loyalty is admirable, but too much lingering on the past can be a liability. You have a mind a mind of your own. You don't need anyone else's approval.

KING OF SWORDS

Your keen imagination will help you become independent. Insecurity, over-sensitivity slows progress. Beware of authority figures and arrogant people. Don't become apathetic or delay developing your talents. Seek the company of those who don't judge you—and, don't judge others at this time. What you think is probably fancy.

Reversed—Be on the lookout for power plays, prejudice, narrow-minded thinking. Jealousy abounds, either yours or another's. You may not be thinking realistically about your own life; make time for repose, relax. Good time for travel with old friends, father-guru types. Trust your intellectual skills, hunches. A fresh viewpoint is essential; don't reject it!

PAGE OF SWORDS

Do you feel that others are intruding in your life? Remember the importance of thinking for yourself, even though you've been conditioned to think like your parents or in older behavior patterns. Exploit your imagination; make a dramatic break from routine, how things have always been. Those who truly love you will stand by you.

Reversed—Are you being silly or childish? Change your course of action, as long as you keep your primary objective in mind. Be wary of friends who make excessive demands unless they give you some consideration of your efforts. And beware of poor eating habits. Not a good time for travel; stick to tried and true, homebase.

KNIGHT OF SWORDS

You're now an understanding listener and know just what to say to please others. However, being so close to associates makes it hard for you to think for yourself. Unless you stand firm in your goals, others may try to gain control over you. Learn to rely on your ability to solve problems; your resources are as valid as other people's.

Reversed—Beware of troublemakers and snoops. Because you dislike conflict, you don't argue when other people disagree with your views. Become less hesitant and bolder. Don't let others dominate your thinking or interfere with developing your talents. Refuse to compromise unless there is no alternative.

SUIT OF WANDS

ACE OF WANDS

It's time for job interviews, dispatching resumes, starting a new business enterprise, or beginning a profitable journey. Your strength uplifts those who lack the resources to solve their problems alone. Be optimistic and courageous. Planning is critical if you're planning to stay a couple of steps ahead of the competition. Say what has to be said to those who should hear it. Learn from past failures, setbacks. Fresh beginnings are on the horizon.

Reversed—Don't be selfish or make false assumptions. Impulsive decisions spell 'disaster.' It pains you not knowing the answers to questions others ask. Cultivate patience, focus, read between the lines of disappointment. Ask for help. Expectations encounter temporary setbacks. Remain strong. There are certain risks worth taking and others that most definitely are not. Be sure you know which is which.

TWO OF WANDS

Be a willing listener. Knowing what people need gives you an advantage over others. Help is on the way, even though you have sufficient self-confidence to succeed where others might fail. Reexamine your goals and define exactly what you want to achieve. The accent is on quality not quantity now; avoid biting off more than you can chew. Tact and perseverance brings rewards.

Reversed—Melancholy, fear, hesitation. Though you may do the right thing and always try to stay within the bounds of acceptable practice, be alert to deception by those who might use you for their own ends. Don't rely too much on loved ones or business associates. No price is too high when it comes to your peace of mind. Trust your instincts, not others.

THREE OF WANDS

Broadcast your talents and opinions; don't hover modestly in the shadows. Be specific about what you want and don't be misled by well-meaning friends. Rewards come when you say what you feel and are willing to cooperate. Teamwork with established friends and associates attracts luck. Believe in yourself and others will share your opinion.

Reversed—Upheavals are a fact of life and can't be avoided. It's how you react to them that matters most. Stop struggling! You're going through the latest in a long line of events designed to test you to see if you have what it takes. Remain focused and don't be intimated by "know-it-alls." Clearly define what you want and refuse to let others intrude. When you reach one goal, another emerges.

FOUR OF WANDS

Making money is nothing to be ashamed of. Open your mind to new ways of improving your finances—take action now! Don't be arrogant or get stuck in old behavior patterns. If you're confused or at a fork in the road, seek options, alternatives. Past efforts bring rewards soon. Work on your credit rating, pay bills. There is much to be learned, but only if you work for it.

Reversed—Allow others to help; assistance is on the way! Appreciate what you have and don't let jealousy or envy get a foot in the door. Look to those who faithfully have stood by you. Errors in judgement are likely now if you allow emotions to cloud reason. Do you really think someone is taking advantage of you? Criticisms over a project appear to be well founded, and if others see matters differently, it is because they lack your close involvement. Speak your mind!

FIVE OF WANDS

People are cranky, and cooperation or morale is low. Keep your chin up! It's possible to speak without saying anything—just as it is not unusual to listen but not hear. There is much to be learned, but only if you work at it. Stay calm during chaos, remember who you are. Tell it like it is, don't be stubborn. Read all fine print: legal entanglements are possible now.

Reversed—We don't always win or come out on top. Accept compromise and apologies. Although you are trying to do your best, current times may be tough. Remember what is truly important. There are good ideas and great ideas. The skill lies in being able to differentiate between them. Now you have a fair chance of turning things your way. Be willing to reprioritize.

SIX OF WANDS

Apologies are in the stars. (Yours?) Have you been looking at matters realistically? Guilt brings all sorts of problems. Competition normally brings out the best in everyone. Don't be afraid to ask questions; don't be smug. Good news is imminent. Convince others that you know what you're talking about. Now's a great time for beginning new health regime, diet.

Reversed—What do you really want or need? Take another look, ask opinions, questions, be suspicious of other's intentions. Are you going to extremes, being moderate? Everyone (including you) wants things "their" way now. Sit things out for now; don't panic or be impatient. Keep matters to yourself before acting. Be grand, discreet.

SEVEN OF WANDS

Faith overcomes current obstacles. Now you have the power to accomplish your goals. Consider all consequences, act swiftly. You are apparently reluctant to reveal your true feelings to someone influential. Not doing so may be the easy solution, but not necessarily the right one. There are ways of expressing your feelings, and once you've learned that, there are significant benefits to be had.

Reversed—Your best strategy is patience—there is much to be learned from the most unlikely sources. Others may deceive or try to use you to satisfy their own objectives, so read between the lines and ask "what's in it for me?" Don't be indecisive or wishy-washy now. Say what you feel and move on. Beware of jealousy, envy. Situations are nowhere near conclusion, so have patience.

EIGHT OF WANDS

Move forward! Plans get the green light now. Your understanding of people and their problems delivers opportunities to get what you want. Friends and nature bring remedies for what ails you. You are now in a position to take control of a family or financial affair and able to convince a relative or business associate that you know what you're talking about.

Reversed—Beware of arguments, jealousy. Energy is scattered, communication cloudy. Think before you act. Partners and loved ones will benefit from your advice—even if it's not what they want to hear. Since they seem to be feeling vulnerable just now, delicacy and diplomacy is essential. When pursuing your objectives, don't ignore the chain of command.

NINE OF WANDS

Fight for, and hold on to what you believe. Projects are near completion, relaxation is near. Victory arrives soon. You can resist the inevitable for only so long, and now you have no alternative but to speak your mind. Others may not agree with what you say, but they will appreciate your frankness. The time is certainly right to feather your own nest for a change.

Reversed—Be prepared, and aware, of the rules of the game. Arrogance creates obstacles. Concentrate on what you do best; this certainly not the time to be rocking the boat. There is more than just pride at stake now. Rid yourself of self-pity, and don't be anxious. This is not the time to reopen old wounds. Take care of your health.

TEN OF WANDS

Earlier attempts to aggressively pursue your ambition results in serious setbacks with superiors if you're not more restrained, honest. Break stubborn patterns, look to new methodologies. An on-the-job transfer is likely now, change of status. Travel for business or pleasure. Whatever decisions you make now, you will have to live with them for months to come, so don't rush into things and make absolutely certain you know what you're dealing with.

Reversed—No changes on the work front. Your body is tightly wound, so pursue health matters now. Unless you focus your energy, it will be wasted. Be sure you have an objective in mind and aren't simply blowing off steam. Return favors to those who've been helpful and be alert to enemy's intentions. Loved ones are under a great deal more pressure than you think, and you could do with a helping hand.

SEVEN OF WANDS

You are now in a determined frame of mind. And if you're going to be determined about anything, it must be boosting your reputation and stabilizing your health. Take the lead, believe in yourself. Dealings with authority figures goes well. Answers arrive when you talk things out with friends and lovers. Write letters, make calls, send faxes. Punctuality counts!

Reversed—Life may have been difficult as of late, but your determination to stick to a task and not be beaten has not gone unnoticed—nor will it go unrewarded. Be willing to change plans, roll with all punches. Bet only what you can afford to lose; don't take silly risks. Unrealistic thinking abounds. Dare to dream, but keep your feet on the ground.

KING OF WANDS

You're capable of success with long-range goals and handling extremely complex situations now. Use intuition and treat others royally. Cooperation brings rewards. Everything seems to be making life difficult, especially where romantic or health affairs are concerned. But is the picture quite as gloomy as you seem to be painting it? Refuse to let sloth or envy overwhelm you.

Reversed—Stay within ethical guidelines, don't be too forceful. You cannot afford to anger or antagonize the wrong people now. What is needed now is not a fresh injection of cash, but a fresh injection of ideas and energy. Seek new options, mobilize your skills. Don't put all your values in material considerations or be intimidated by other's possessions or performances.

PAGE OF WANDS

Be tactful and diplomatic. People respond to generosity and are in a "giving" mode now. Ask for assistance, get matters off your chest. Refuse to be rushed. Forgive and forget. Whatever you want most out of life—be it success or recognition—you now stand every chance of getting it. However, you now have to decide how much you are prepared to spend.

Reversed—Your enthusiasm is liable to run ahead of you by leaps and bounds, and at times you may find it difficult keeping pace with your own ideas. Everyone wants to get things done quickly now. Don't overlook important details. Folks are lazy; just earn your keep. Bury the hatchet and refuse to let old issues interfere with today's happiness.

KNIGHT OF WANDS

The more assured you are the better things will go. Everyone is playing to win; be prepared for competition. Fight the need to have the final word. Take some chances, talk things out.

Reversed—Don't believe everything you hear. Beware of impatience and others' white lies. Don't get pulled into matters you dislike, lots of ego posturing in the air. Stand firm in your convictions and know when to swallow your pride. Before you throw good money after bad, consider what you are trying to achieve. The time is long past when you can spend your way out of trouble.

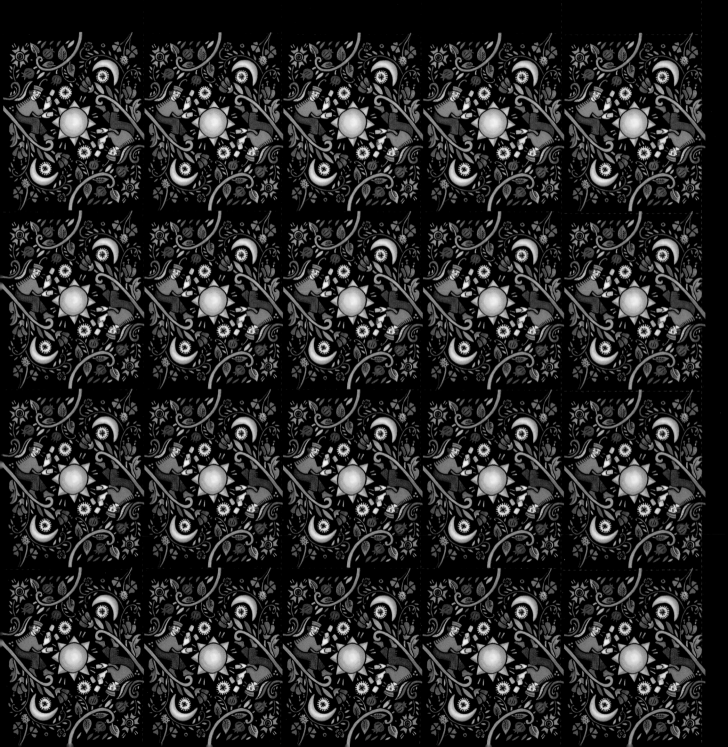

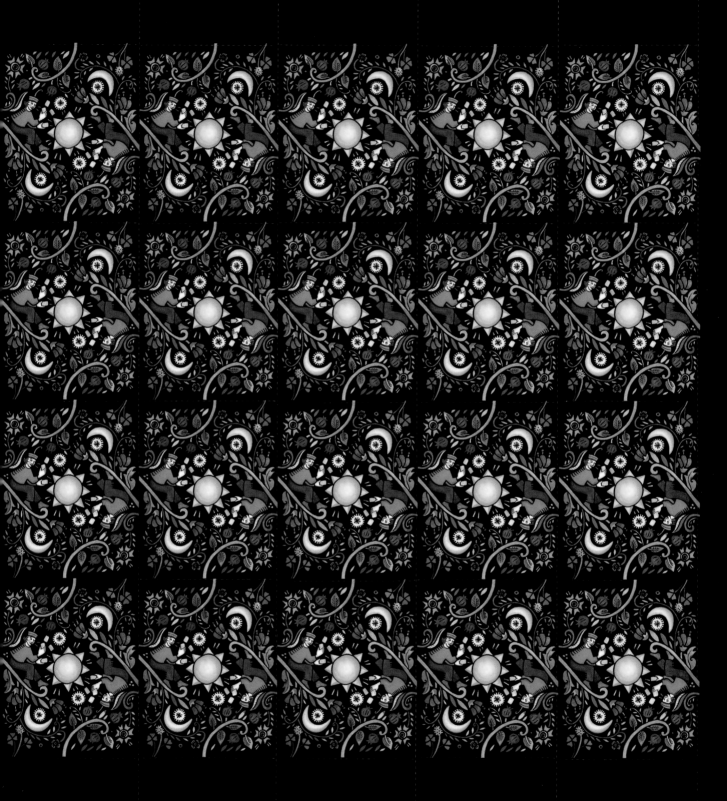

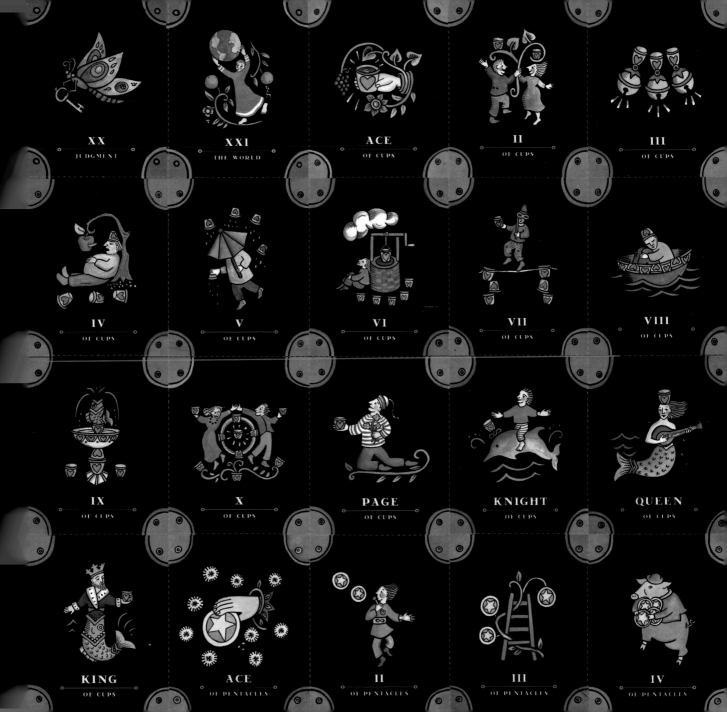

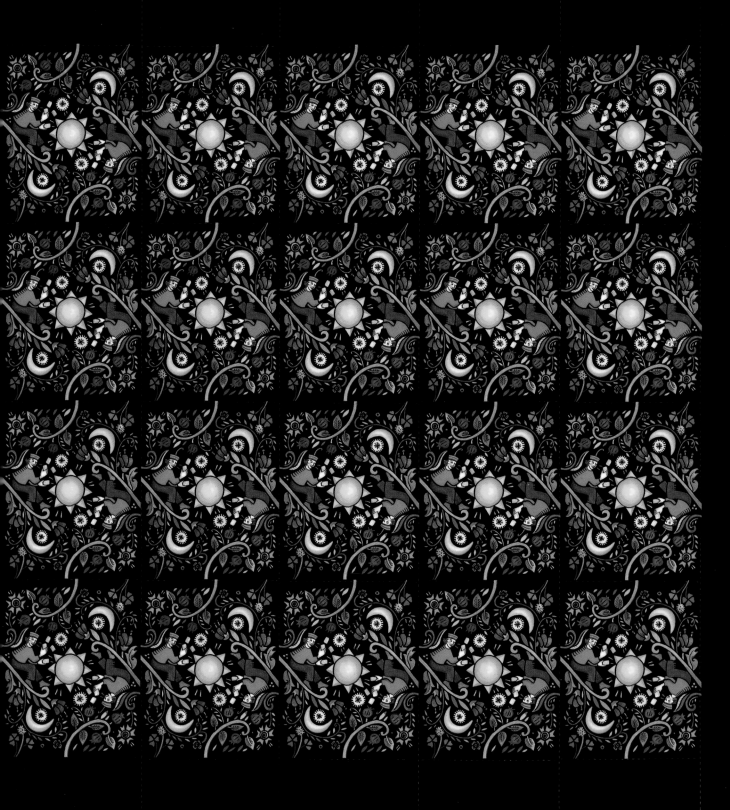

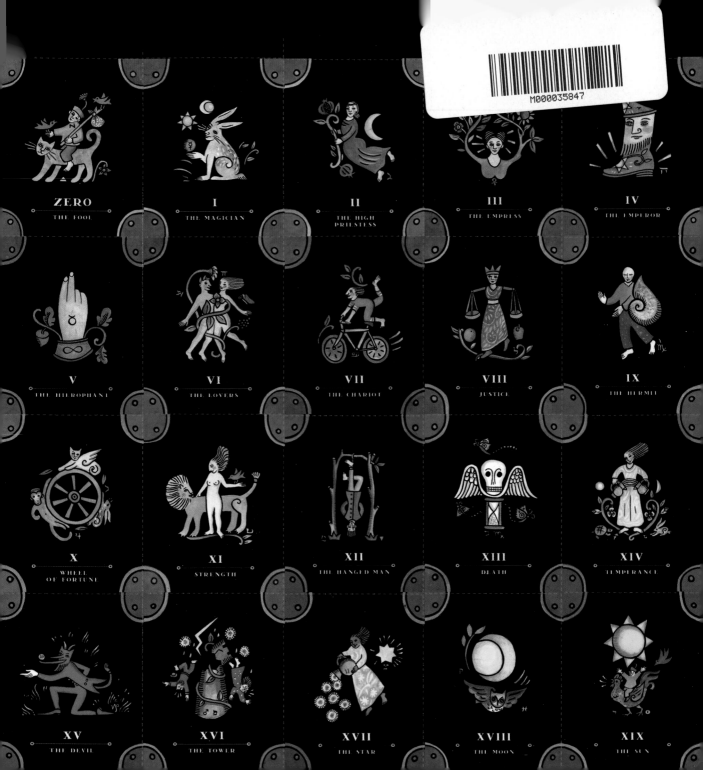

ZERO — THE FOOL

I — THE MAGICIAN

II — THE HIGH PRIESTESS

III — THE EMPRESS

IV — THE EMPEROR

V — THE HIEROPHANT

VI — THE LOVERS

VII — THE CHARIOT

VIII — JUSTICE

IX — THE HERMIT

X — WHEEL OF FORTUNE

XI — STRENGTH

XII — THE HANGED MAN

XIII — DEATH

XIV — TEMPERANCE

XV — THE DEVIL

XVI — THE TOWER

XVII — THE STAR

XVIII — THE MOON

XIX — THE SUN